THE YOUTH'S BOOK ON NATURAL THEOLOGY

THE YOUTH'S BOOK
ON
NATURAL THEOLOGY
ILLUSTRATED

IN FAMILIAR DIALOGUES

Thomas H. Gallaudet

Solid Ground Christian Books
Birmingham, Alabama USA

Solid Ground Christian Books
PO Box 660132
Vestavia Hills, AL 35266
205-443-0311
sgcb@charter.net
http://solid-ground-books.com

The Youth's Book on the Natural Theology

Thomas H. Gallaudet (1787-1851)

Taken from 1832 edition by The American Tract Society, NY

Solid Ground Classic Reprints

First printing of new edition October 2007

Cover work by Borgo Design, Tuscaloosa, AL
Contact them at **borgogirl@bellsouth.net**

Cover image is taken from an engraving in the original edition

ISBN: 1-59925-128-0

CONTENTS.

	Page.
Preface.	5
Address to Young Readers.	8

DIALOGUE 1.—Explanation of *skill*, contrivance and design. The Nautilus and Steam-boat., . . 11

DIAL. 2.—God the great designer and contriver. How does God show himself to us? 23

DIAL. 3.—The pencil-case. The arm and hand. A description of the bones and joints of the arm. Atheists. Chance. 32

DIAL. 4.—Joint at the shoulder. Muscles and tendons. Joint at the elbow. 44

DIAL. 5.—Radius. Ulna. Button-head. Joint-oil. Gristle. Ligament. Wisdom and goodness of God. 55

DIAL. 6.—God does not design and contrive as we do. The skill of God explained. The wrist and hand. 66

DIAL. 7.—What makes the bones move or the joints. The muscles. The tendons. Contraction of the muscles. 78

DIAL. 8.—Antagonist muscles. The nerves. Nerves of expression in the human countenance. Their use. A sound muscle. 91

DIAL. 9.—Another sound muscle. The eyelid. Shedding tears. Parts of the body *keep on* going right. Nerves of the face. Expressions of the countenance compared with a painting. . . . 103

DIAL. 10.—More on the expression of the countenance. Goodness and wisdom of God. Habits of expression. 117

DIAL. 11.—The elephant. The eye of a dragon-fly. The trunk of an elephant. Pressure of the air. 127

CONTENTS.

Dial. 12.—Mouth of animals; particular design in forming them. Wood-pecker. Cross-bill. Bills of ducks and geese. Oyster-catcher. Chœtodon. Chance. Atheism. 139

Dial. 13.—The electrical eel. Lightning. Electricity. Dr. Franklin. 153

Dial. 14.—Sting of the bee. Mouths of insects. Moths and butterflies. Their tongues. The pump. The eggs of the butterfly. Caterpillar. Chrysalis. Butterfly. The resurrection. 164

Dial. 15.—How different insects deposit their eggs. The butterfly. The moth. The gad-fly. Ants. The queen ant. The workers. The grubs. The pupæ. The cocoons. Birds' nests. Bee-hives. . . 177

Dial. 16.—Instincts. Sprouting of seed. Plant called the *fly-trap*. Explanation of what *instinct* is. Design, wisdom and goodness of God. Reason distinguished from instinct. 189

Dial. 17.—Proportion, a proof of design. Proportion between our bodies and the things around us. Proportion between animals and plants. Proportion between animals and their habitations. A statue. St. Peter's Church. God the great statuary. God the great architect. 203

Dial. 18.—The air and lungs; the heart, arteries and veins adapted to each other. The atmosphere. Hearing. The ear. Its parts. Hearing explained. The circulation of the blood. Adaptation a proof of design. The air. Light explained. The air adapted to the eye. Light. Light adapted to the eye. Wonderful power, wisdom and goodness of God. 213

Conclusion.—Address to the conscience of youth. . 225

PREFACE.

Some may deem it almost unnecessary, to go into an argument, with children and youth, to prove to them, that there is a God: a truth, which seems, too often, to be *taken for granted*, not only in the first stages, but through the whole course, of their religious instruction—how wisely, may admit of very serious doubts.

It is a truth, on which all the doctrines and precepts of religion rest; and just in proportion as the belief of it is weak, or obscure, will all the other truths of religion, fail to have their full effect upon the heart and the life.

This, like other truths, is *founded on evidence*. The more complete, therefore, and satisfactory, this evidence is; the more thoroughly it is considered and examined; the more it is made to form a part of the customary trains of thought and feeling; and the more distinct and vivid the conceptions are, which it produces in the mind;—the more uniform and operative, will be the belief of the truth which this evidence is intended to establish.

This we find to be the case, even with regard to those truths which are the most common, and which receive the uniform assent of every intelligent mind.

For the practical belief of truth, is very much strengthened by a knowledge of the nature and certainty of its evidence, and by *the habit of frequently recurring to this evidence.*

After attending to the various, and interesting, and overwhelming proofs of design, contrivance, and skill, in all that we see, within us, and around us,—who can fail to have the existence and agency of God, impressed upon his understanding and heart, with new freshness and force.

Let these proofs form a part of the early associations of thought and feeling, among children and youth; and, from the well known laws of the human mind, the important truth which they establish, will so blend itself with the habitudes of the soul, that God will be seen in all HIS works, and HIS presence felt in the exhibitions which HE is continually making to us, of HIS power, wisdom, and goodness.

Besides, atheism, theoretical, and practical, is on the alert, to diffuse its baleful influence. Already, in our own country, we have seen it attempting to make proselytes. Debating societies, public lectures, books, tracts, and newspapers, have been the instruments employed for its propagation. What parent can tell how soon his child may be exposed to this awful delusion? Who that knows the waywardness of the human heart; the force of temptation; the insidious allurements of vice; the gradual encroachment which sneers and ridicule on the one hand, and sceptical queries and doubts on the other, often make upon the conscience, *especially when this conscience seeks relief from the wounds that guilt has inflicted upon it;*—who that considers these things, can fail to tremble, often, at the exposure of our youth to this contaminating influence of infidelity and atheism?

It has, already, in not a few instances, withered and

blasted the fondest hopes of the anxious father and mother. If it does not always destroy, it may often paralyze, religious belief.

And, if the faith of the youth is secure against its attacks, still, how much good, often, this very faith may do, in rescuing others. If it is thoroughly furnished with evidence, and arguments and proofs, its triumphs, both in private and in public, may save a companion from ruin, and hasten the downfall of this bitter enemy of God and man.

For these reasons, the author cannot but think, that the evidences of the existence of God, are quite too much overlooked in the early religious education of children and youth. He could wish, for one, that they might form a part of the regular course of instruction in Sabbath Schools, and of the religious reading in families. The subject may be made deeply interesting. Many of the *facts* connected with it, are as really *entertaining* as most of the incidents in the books of *religious fiction*, with which children have been so extensively supplied. They are vastly more *instructive;* and tend, too, to form a *taste for useful knowledge*, which, if confirmed into a habit, is of unspeakable value.

The author will only add, that having intended what he has written for quite young persons, he has gone into a minuteness of analysis, and a specification of details, which, his own experience has fully convinced him, is the only sure mode of conveying distinct ideas to those, whose powers of generalizing are but, as yet, very imperfectly cultivated and developed.

TO MY YOUNG READERS.

I dare say, many of you who are not more than eight, or ten years of age, will be able to understand this book;—particularly, if you are very attentive in reading it, and if you, always, ask some older person to explain to you a few things, which, at first, may be difficult to be understood.

Those who are a few years older, will I think, find no difficulty at all, in understanding it.

You may not, however, know exactly the meaning of the term, *Natural Theology*, which forms a part of the title of the book. I will endeavor to explain it to you.

Theology is an English word, made by putting two Greek words together, with a little alteration. *Theo*, comes from the Greek word *Theos*, which means *God;* and *logy*, from the Greek word, *logos*, which means *a discourse, or speaking, or teaching, about any thing*.

All that is known about God,—arranged in order, so that it can be taught clearly, and distinctly,—is called *Theology*.

In the Bible, God has made known to men, a great deal about himself, which they did not know before, and which they could not have learned in any other way; or, what means the same thing, *he has revealed the knowledge of himself to them, in the Bible.*

The Bible is a revelation from God; and from what it teaches us about him, we gain *that knowledge*, which, when arranged in order, so that it can be taught clearly and distinctly, is called *revealed Theology*.

Natural Theology is not learned from the Bible. It

is all that can be known about God, merely by examining the beings and things which he has made, without the aid of revealed Theology.

The beings and things which God has made, and causes to be, or live and grow, are called *natural*, to distinguish them from the things that men make.

The things that men make, are called, *works of art;* but all that God has made, we call, the *works of nature.* By examining and studying the works of nature, we can see, that there must be a God, who made, and preserves, all beings, and things; and we can learn many things about him, which will show us his great power and wisdom, and goodness.

All the knowledge which we can thus gain, about God, is called, *Natural Theology;* and it is this knowledge, my young friends, which I wish, in some degree, to give you, in this book that I have written for you. I hope, you will be so much interested in gaining this knowledge, that you will seek for more of it, as you grow older, in larger books which have been written on the same subject, but which it might, now, be difficult for you to understand.

I have written the book in dialogues, between a lady, whom I call Mrs. Stanhope, and her son, Robert. If any of you have read *the Child's book on the Soul*, it is the same Robert who is mentioned there, only, in this book, he is supposed to be a few years older.

That you may all make great improvement in useful knowledge, and especially in the knowledge of God, and of your duty, and learn, both *to be good, and to do good*, is the sincere wish of

Your friend,
THE AUTHOR.

THE YOUTH'S BOOK

ON

NATURAL THEOLOGY.

DIALOGUE I.

Mother. Did you ever *make* any thing, Robert?

Robert. I made a *kite*, once, mother, and it flew very well. Uncle John showed me *how* to make it.

M. Out of *what* did you make it?

R. Out of paper, and sticks, and thread.

M. *How* did you put them together?

R. With some paste; and then, I let the kite dry in the sun, and put the tail on, and fixed the twine to it, and it was all ready to fly.

M. *How long* did it take you to make it?

R. I should think, almost two hours, mother. I spoiled one or two, before I got right. I think I could make one now, a good deal quicker.

M. Do you remember that beautiful large kite which the boys raised, in front of the school house, last spring?

R. Yes, it was as tall as a man. It took several boys to hold it, when it was high up in the air.

M. Do you know who made it?

R. Some one of the boys, I suppose, mother; but I do not know which.

M. Are you sure, that one of the boys made it?

R. I think so; but perhaps some man made it, it was so large and strong.

M. Are you sure that *any body* made it?

R. Yes, mother, just as sure as I am that *I made* the little kite that we were talking about. Somebody must-have cut the paper; and cut out the sticks right, and tied them together; and put the thread round; and pasted the paper; and fixed on the tail; or the kite never would have been made.

M. Yes, my son, and the tail must have been made *just long and heavy enough*, or the kite would not have flown.

R. I remember, mother, I made the tail to my kite *too short*, first; and as soon as it got a little way up into the air, it began to go round and round, and fell down to the ground. It would not fly at all, till I made the tail longer.

M. I suppose, Robert, that some boys have made kites so often, that they can make a very good kite *at once*, without any mistake.

R. Yes, mother, I am pretty sure that I could.

M. If you could, my son, and make it quick, and exactly right, so that it would fly very well, you would be said to be *skilful* in making a kite. And as it flew finely in the air, it would show your *skill* in making it.

R. Mother, it takes most skill to fix the tail.

M. I suppose so. And you have to *think beforehand*, do you not, of what shape you will make the kite; and then, how much paper it will take; and how many sticks there must be; and how you will tie them together ; so as to make the kite of just the shape and size that you want ?

R. Oh, yes, mother. I have to think all about that. For, you know, we can make kites of many different sizes and shapes. I should have to *think a great deal beforehand*, how to make a kite like that tall one which the boys had.

M. Yes; and perhaps you would have to get your uncle John to *think for you.*

R. I think I should, mother.

M. Well, if your uncle John should think beforehand *how to make the kite*, and tell you how to go to work, and do exactly every thing that ought to be done; he would *contrive* the kite. When it was done, it would show *your skill* in making it; and it would show *his contrivance*, in thinking beforehand *how it* should be made.

R. Mother, I can contrive a little kite. Will you let me make one this afternoon ?

M. Yes; after you have said your lessons. What will you make the kite *for ?*

R. I will make it to *fly*, mother. What else should I make it for ? You do not think, I would make a kite just to look at.

M. I did not know, Robert, but you would make one to show me that you could *contrive* a kite, and that you had skill to make one.

R. But how could I show that, mother, if the kite would not *fly well?* No; I should make the kite *on purpose to fly.* And, indeed, I was not thinking at all about making it, to show you my *contrivance* or *skill.*

M. Your purpose, or *design,* then, in making the kite, would be, that it might fly well.

What was your *design,* in making that little boat, the other day? What did you make it for?

R. My *design* was, that it might swim in the small pond, back of the garden.

M. Did you make it, as you do a kite?

R. Oh, no mother. You know a boat swims in *water,* but a kite flies in the *air.*

M. Which did you have to contrive most about, in making,—the boat or the kite?

R. I think, the kite, mother, for the tail troubled me a good deal, before I got it exactly right.

M. What if you should get your uncle John, to make a boat large enough to carry you; and then fasten the string of the kite to it, when it was high up in the air; and so the kite draw you in the boat, quite across the pond. How prettily you would sail.

R. Yes, mother. But the kite would have to be a very large one, and uncle John would have to think a long time to *contrive* it, and to be very *skilful* in fixing it all right, so as to make the boat go.

M. There is a little fish, which is a great deal more curious than such a boat and kite would be.

R. Do tell me about it, mother. What is it called?

M. It is called a *nautilus*. Nautilus is a word, that used to be spoken by a people who spoke very differently from us, a great many years ago, and it means *a sailor*.

R. Why? does this little fish sail in a boat?

M. Yes, my son, and it lives in the same boat in which it swims and sails.

R. What is the boat made of?

M. The boat is a thin shell round and hollow. It is as thin as paper, and very light, so that it will float on the top of the water, just as your little boat does. The shell is a part of the fish; and inside of the shell is *the living part*, soft and slimy, like a snail. It is a good deal softer than the inside, and living part, of an oyster.

When this little fish wishes to sail, it raises up two short arms which it has; and between these arms, there is something stretched, very thin, like a web, which the wind blows, and so away it sails, on the top of the water.

It has, also, two other arms which it lets down into the water, on each side of the shell; and it paddles with them; and makes itself go along faster;

and turns itself with them, and goes one way or another, as it chooses.

You know if you fill your little boat with water, it will sink. So, when the nautilus, about which I have been telling you, wishes to go down into the deep water, it first draws in its two arms that have the sail between them, and the other two that it paddles with. Then it has a way of drawing in the water, and filling all the inside of the shell, which makes it so heavy, that it sinks away down to the bottom, like a stone.

When it wishes to rise again, it throws out the water through the little holes of which its arms are full, and makes itself light, and soon it rises, and keeps rising, till it reaches the top of the water.

When the weather is pleasant, and the water smooth, the people that are in the ships on the great ocean, often see a great many of these little shell fish, or *sailors in their boats*, with their sails up, and sailing all about, as happy as can be. But if the wind blows hard, or any thing disturbs them, they take in their sails, and draw in their arms, and fill themselves with water, and away they go, down into the deep ocean, and are not seen again for some time.

R. Mother, I never heard of such a curious thing before. It is, indeed, a great deal more curious than a boat would be, large enough to carry me, with a kite fixed to it, so that I could sail across the pond. How large is the nautilus?

M. A gentleman told me, who had seen one, that it was about as large as a bowl which he could hold in his two hands. But it was not shaped like a bowl.

Here is a picture of one, as it appears when its sail

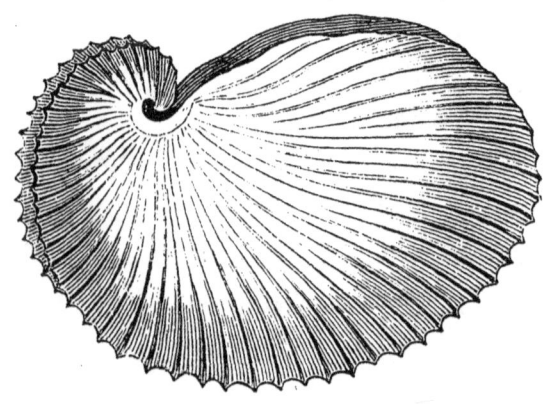

and arms are all drawn inside of the shell. I could not find a true picture of one as it appears when it is sailing.

R. Oh! I wish I had a little nautilus, mother.

M. Suppose you ask your uncle John to make you one; he knows how to make a great many curious things.

R. He could not make one, mother. He would not know what to make the *shell* of.

ON NATURAL THEOLOGY. 19

M. Suppose, somebody should give him the shell of a nautilus. Could he not make *the other parts*, and put them inside of it?

R. Perhaps he might make something like the *sail*, mother. But how could he make the two little arms that carry the sail, and the two arms that paddle, and make them stretch themselves out, and draw themselves in? Besides, the little nautilus is *alive*. Uncle John, if he were to make something almost exactly like the nautilus, *could not make it live*, so as to move itself about, and go down under the water, and rise up again, just as it chooses.

M. Suppose your uncle John had never seen a nautilus, or heard about one, and should make something almost exactly like one; and fix some little wheels inside, like those inside of a watch, and have a spring to make the wheels go; and then wind it up with a key, and put it on the water; and it should raise up its sail, and work with its paddles, and sail away, for some time, a good deal as a nautilus does. Would you not wonder at your uncle John's *contrivance*, and at his *skill* too?

R. I should, indeed, mother. But do you suppose, that any body has *contrivance and skill enough* to make such a little nautilus?

M. When you was in the steamboat, Robert, you was in something like a *great nautilus*. Do you not remember how many, many wheels there were, and iron things that moved up and down, and many different ways.

I showed you the wooden wheels, like paddles, on each side of the boat, going round and round in the water, and told you that it was the *other wheels* that made *them* go, and move the boat along.

It must have taken a great deal of *contrivance and skill*, to make a steamboat ; and, perhaps, the man that contrived the *steamboat*, might also contrive a *little nautilus*, with wheels inside of it, to sail on the water.

R. You have forgotten, mother, that the steamboat did not hoist any sail up, as the nautilus does. I think *that part* of the nautilus would be very difficult to *contrive*. And, then, I do not believe any body could have *contrivance and skill enough*, to make it take in its sail, and its arms, and fill itself with water ; and go down to the bottom, and afterwards, come up again.

It would puzzle uncle John, and every body else, even the man that contrived the steamboat! to do *that*.

M. Well, I think it would, Robert. And for any body to make a *live nautilus*, you know, that would be *impossible*.

R. Yes, mother, and *I am astonished at the wonderful contrivance and skill which we see in the nautilus!*

M. So am I, my son. The more I think of it, the more I wonder at it.

If you should live a thousand years; and study ever so much; and make thousands and thousands of curious things; you never would have contrivance and skill enough, to make any thing so wonderful as a *live nautilus*.

R. Mother, *nobody can make a live thing, that will move of itself.*

M. That is true, Robert. But, it is almost time for us to end our conversation. I wish, however, to ask you, first, one or two questions.

You said, that you would make a little kite, *on purpose* to fly, and I told you that it would be your *design*, in making it, to have it fly.

If you had seen a nautilus out of the water, without ever having seen it before, or heard any thing about it, do you think, you could tell what its different parts were *designed* for?

R. I think I could, mother. The shell would look so like a little boat; and there would be something so like a sail; and the two little paddles, on each side; that I am sure, I should think it was to go and move on the water. I should know it would not be, to fly in the air, or to crawl on the ground.

M. And if you should see it *hoist up* its little sail, and put out, and move, its little arms, like paddles;

you would feel quite certain, that *the design* was, that it should sail about on the top of the water—would you not?

R. I should, mother.

M. Well, you see, my son, not only that there is wonderful contrivance and skill, in the different parts of the nautilus, but a *wonderful design*, too, in putting these parts together, and having them act upon each other just as they do.

If the nautilus had not a way of throwing out the water, and rising to the top, it could not sail on the top of the water; and there would be no use in having *any* of its parts so as to help it to sail.

If the shell were not thin and round and hollow, it could not float, even after it rises to the top of the water.

There would be no use, in its raising up its arms, and stretching them out, if there were not a thin, web-like something between them, as a sail, for the wind to blow against.

And it would do but little good to hoist its sail, and be blown about, if it could not guide itself by the two little paddles, and so determine which way to go.

And it would not be best for it, to come up to the top of the water, and sail about, if it could not make itself sink, and go down again, when there is danger.

You see what a wonderful thing the nautilus is!

DIALOGUE II.

Robert. I have thought a good deal, mother, about the nautilus. I want to see one, very much.

Mother. If you should ever go on the ocean, in a ship, when you grow up to be a man, you will, probably, see many of them.

But there are some things which you see every day, which are as curious as the nautilus is.

R. Mother, a *chicken* is a curious little animal.

M. Yes, my son; and if you could look *inside* of a chicken, you would find a great many parts, quite as curious as the sail and paddles of the nautilus.

And you would see as much *wonderful design*, in the way in which these parts are put together, and what they are made for.

Look, too, at the outside of a chicken. Stroke its little feathers. How smooth, and light, and warm they are. What a good *covering* they are, for the little creature. How many feathers there are, all lying one way, and every feather itself is very curious.

The *mouth* of a chicken is very different from the mouth of a dog, or of a cat. It has a long bill, made sharp, and it opens so that it can pick up the corn and little seeds, very easily, like a pair of nippers.

It has claws, too, just right for scratching in the ground, to find its food; and for keeping fast hold of the branch of a tree, when it grows older, and goes there to roost, at night.

I think, a chicken has as many curious parts as the nautilus.

R. I do not know but it has, mother; and I think, it would be a great deal more difficult for any body to make a little chicken, with wheels inside, so that it could walk, and scratch in the ground, and pick up corn and seeds, than it would be to make a nautilus that would sail.

M. It would be so, my son.

But now I wish to explain something to you, that is more wonderful than any thing which I have yet told you, about the nautilus or the chicken.

Suppose, your uncle John could make a nautilus, with so many new and curious wheels inside of it, that somehow or other, these wheels would move, and, by and by, make another nautilus, *just like the first*.

And, suppose, there should be wheels, inside of this second one, that should move in the same way, and make a third; and so on, till a hundred were made.

R. Mother, you know that uncle John, or any body else, could never do that.

M. But, only suppose that he could, my son. Would you not think, that his contrivance and skill would be a thousand times more wonderful, than if he made only *one nautilus?*

R. Certainly, mother, I should.

M. Well, Robert, there is *something like this*, with regard to the little chicken.

You know, the hen lays eggs. She hatches them, and the little chickens come out of the eggs. When the chickens grow up, *they* lay eggs, and hatch more little chickens. And so they keep on, year after year.

R. How many years ago did the *first hen* live, mother?

M. Oh! a great many years ago. Do you not think, that there was wonderful contrivance, and skill, and design, shown in that *first hen?*

R. I do, indeed, mother. For that first hen laid eggs, and little chickens came out of them; and, then, these chickens grew up, and laid more eggs; and more chickens came out of them, and so on, till what a wonderful number of chickens there have been in the world.

M. Yes, my son. You see that there is a great deal of *contrivance and skill* shown in a little chicken, and a great deal of *design*, in the way in which all its parts are put together. You see, too, that all this contrivance and skill, and design, was shown, *still more wonderfully, in the first hen.*

Now, when you look at a kite, you know with what design it was made, and you see the contrivance and skill with which its parts were put together. You know, *that somebody must have made it, and have thought, beforehand, how to make it. The kite could not have made itself.*

So, when you look at the curious little chicken, or the curious little nautilus, and see the wonderful design, and skill, and contrivance which are shown in them, *you know, that some one must have made them, and have made the first hen, and the first nautilus,* and have thought, beforehand, *how* to make them.

It is your *spirit*, your *mind*, which thinks beforehand, which designs, and contrives, and directs your hands to be *skillful*, whenever you make a kite.

It is **GOD**, *the* **GREAT SPIRIT**, *the* **ETERNAL MIND**, *who thought beforehand, who designed, contrived, and made every little chicken and nautilus, and the first hen and nautilus; and the first things and beings, and all things and beings.*

When you see, my son, such *wonderful skill and contrivance* in the thousand beings and things which are around you, and the *design* with which they were made, and all their parts put together; you know, certainly, that *there is a* **GOD** *who made them,* just as certainly as you know, that the tall

ON NATURAL THEOLOGY. 27

kite which you saw the boys playing with, must have been made by somebody.

GOD shows himself to you; he shows you his wonderful knowledge, and contrivance, and power, and skill, and design in your own body and soul, which he made, and in all the beings and things which are around you.

R. How does God show Himself to me, mother? *I do not see him.*

M. Do you see *me*, Robert?

R. Yes, mother, I see you now, sitting right before me.

M. When I am *asleep*, can you see me then?

R. Certainly; I saw you last evening, mother, when you was so tired, and slept in your chair.

M. Suppose, I should *die*, could you see me then?

R. I should see your dead body.

M. But the *dead body* would not be *myself*. It would not be *your mother*, whom you now see, and who is talking to you. My soul, or spirit, would have left the body; and if any one should ask you, where your mother was, you would say, you hoped, that *she* had gone to heaven.

Look at my spectacles. When you see *them* do you see *me?*

R. No, mother, but I see *you* looking through them.

M. When you look at my *eyes*, do you see me?

R. I see *you*, mother, looking through them.

M. So, when you see my lips and tongue move, you see *me*, speaking to you with them. And when you see any part of my body moving, you see *me* making it move.

When I am awake, you see my *waking body*. When I am asleep, you see my *sleeping body*. And if I should die, you would see my *dead body*. **But you cannot see my soul.**

It is my soul which is now looking at you, through *the eyes* of the body. It is my soul which is now speaking to you, with the *lips and tongue* of the body. When I rise and walk, or do any thing with my hands, it is my soul which does it, with the *feet and hands* of the body.

My body, with all its parts, so curiously and wonderfully made, is a *kind of machine*, or a collection of instruments, which my soul uses, in different ways, to do the different things which I wish to do.

R. I remember, mother, you told me once about your spectacles being like *another pair of eyes*.

M. Yes, my son. My spectacles are an instrument, which I use, to help me to see better. A man made them, and they are curiously made.

So my eyes are instruments which I use, to see with; and my tongue is an instrument which I use to talk with; and my hands are instruments which I use, to do a great many things with. GOD made my eyes, my tongue, and my hands; and they are vastly more curious instruments than any man can make.

R. So they are, mother, and they are a great deal better, too; for they do not get out of order. as other instruments do; and we can carry them about with us, without any trouble.

M. Do you remember that curious machine, Robert, which I took you to see, the other day, in the cotton factory?

R. I do, mother; how full it was of little wheels, and a great many curious things, that kept moving so many different ways.

M. Did you see what made it move?

R. No, mother. But you told me, there was a boy in the other room, turning a large wheel, which made the machine move.

M. If you should go there again, and see the machine moving, what would you think made it move?

R. I should *know*, that it was a boy, in the other room, made it move.

M. So, when you see any part of my body, which is itself a very curious machine, moving, or doing any thing, you know that it is my soul, (like the boy, in the other room,) making it move and do so.

R. Yes, mother, only I can open the door, and go into the other room, and *see the boy*, but I cannot find out any way to see your soul.

M. Neither would you see the *boy's soul.* You would only see his body, and his arm and hand moving, which turn the machine. You say you *see me*, because my soul, or, what is the same thing, *myself*, is shown to you, through, or with, my body. You would not know, that I was in my body, if I did not show myself to you, by making my body move, or do something. If I did not open my eyes, but lay perfectly still, and did not move at all, and lay so for several days, you would think that I was dead, and that I was no longer in my body. You would not say, that you saw me.

R. I begin to understand you, mother.

M. Well, as you cannot see *my spirit*, only as I show myself to you, through, or with, my body ; so you cannot see GOD, the Great Spirit, only as *he shows himself* to you, in the wonderful things which he has made.

When I open my eyes, and *look at you kindly*, you say, *you see me* looking at you kindly: and you love me, and call me your dear mother.

When the sun shines pleasantly over the eastern hills *on you*, and on every thing around you ; and you look at it, and rejoice in its cheerful light ;—

think, that it is GOD who makes it shine so pleasantly, and that you can, as it were, *see him looking kindly at you*, and love him, and call him your heavenly Father.

R. Yes, mother, and when I see the beautiful, clear moon, and the bright stars, I can think too, that I see GOD looking down upon me from the blue sky.

M. When I *speak* to you, my son, you love to hear my voice, and you say, that you *hear me speaking to you*.

You sometimes, hear the wind gently blowing, through the trees, and making a pleasant sound among the leaves.

Is it not the voice of GOD? You do, as it were, *hear him speaking kindly to you;* and you must love him.

R. Mother, I sometimes hear it thunder, and I am afraid. *Does GOD speak to me then?*

M. Why not, my son, and why should you be afraid?

It is GOD who makes the forked lightning, and loud thunder. *He* directs the storm, and he can keep you as safe in the midst of it, as when the sky is all clear and pleasant.

It is *his voice* that you hear in the thunder. You hear him, as it were, *speaking to you from the dark clouds.* He tells you, that it is he who thunders in the heavens; that he is Almighty, and that you must fear to displease him; *that he is Almighty,* and that he can do all things as he chooses; that *in his hands* you are safe, and that he will make you happy with him forever, in that bright and beautiful heaven, away above the dark clouds where it is thundering, if you will love and obey him.

R. Mother, how many new and strange things you have told me! How great and wonderful GOD is! When will you tell me more about him, and *how he shows himself to me in the things which he has made?*

M. I will teach you about him again, my son, very soon. In the meanwhile, remember what I have already taught you.

And as you are learning more and more of GOD, you should desire to love him, more and more; to think, and speak of him, more and more; and to obey him, more and more.

DIALOGUE III.

Mother. What is *contrivance*, Robert?
Robert. *It is to think beforehand, how to make any thing.*

M. Can you tell me of something, which it required a good deal of contrivance to make?

R. Yes, mother, your silver pencil-case.

M. You are right, Robert. You see it has a little hole at one end, to keep the lead pencils in. And one part at the other end unscrews and comes off, so that you can put a pencil into it. Then, there is another screw, and a small wire, which pushes the little pencil out, every time that you turn the screw. It is very curious. I do not have to sharpen my pencil with a pen-knife, as I used to do. I think it is a great deal more convenient than the old kind of pencils, which I had to sharpen with a pen-knife. The man that first thought how to make it, must have had *a good deal of contrivance.*

Now, Robert, tell me what *skill* is.

R. I remember, mother, you told me, yesterday. It is, after any body has contrived how to make any thing,—to get every thing ready, and put all the parts together, just as they ought to be, so as to have the thing well made, and to do all this, easily and exactly, without making any mistake. I think, there is a good deal of skill shown, in making, and putting together, all the parts of your silver pencil-case.

M. What do you understand, by *design?*

R. The man who contrived and made the first pencil-case, like your's, mother thought, *what he would make it for*,—to hold a little lead pencil, which would not need sharpening, and with which you could write a great deal more conveniently than with the old kind. This was his *design* in making it. *Design is to think beforehand what we will make a thing for.*

M. I am glad, my son, to see, that you understand, and recollect so well, what I have taught you.

Now tell me, can a very curious and useful instrument be made, to do a particular thing with, unless somebody first has a *design;* and *contrives* it; and makes it *skilfully;* so as to have it just right for doing *that particular thing?*

R. Certainly not, mother.

M. Robert, if you should see such an instrument, very convenient to do a particular thing with, having a great many curious parts, all put together just right for the instrument to be used easily and well, would you not know, that it must have been *contrived* and made by some very *skilful* person, who had a particular *design* in making it?

R. I certainly should, mother.

M. Well, my son, I am going to show you such an instrument; so curiously and wonderfully made; with so much design, and contrivance, and skill, in it; so much more curious and wonderful than any thing that a man can make; that you will see in it, GOD, who designed it, showing his great wisdom, and power, and goodnes to you.

This instrument alone, is enough to convince us, that there is a GOD.

R. Do show me this instrument, mother, I wish to see it very much.

M. Lay your arm on this table, Robert, and keep your elbow still.

Now turn your hand over. Turn it back again. Turn it over and back again, a good many times, very quickly.

Now bend your elbow, and raise your hand up, so as to touch your shoulder. Let it fall again. Raise it and let it fall again, a good many times, very quickly.

Now make your thumb and fingers move, as many different ways as you can.

Now stretch out your whole arm as far as you can. Do not bend it at all. Swing it round and round, and make it go up and down, and to the right and to the left, as far as you can, and as fast as you can.

Your arm and hand, my son, is the instrument which I was going to show you.

Must it not be very curiously made, that you can make so many different kinds of motions with it.

R. It must, indeed, mother; do explain to me, more about it.

M. I will, my son, and you will see how kind GOD is, in providing you with such an instrument, with which you can do so many different things.

Did you ever think, how many different things we can do with our arms and hands?

R. I never did, mother; but I now begin to think about it, and to wonder at it.

M. We can do so many things with our arms and hands, that I have not time to tell you about them all.

Only look around you, and see the people who are busy and industrious; how many thousand, thousand different things they can do with their arms and hands!

By the help of their arms and hands, people build houses to live in. They make clothes to wear. They plough, and sow, and reap, and gather in the grain, and vegetables, and fruits. They prepare food, in a great many different ways, to eat. They spin, weave, paint, carve, engrave, print, and write.

But this is not one half, no, not one thousandth part, of what people do with their arms and hands.

How helpless and miserable we should be, if we had no arms and hands; or if they were made just like the leg and foot of a dog, or horse; or like the leg and claw of a bird.

R. All that you are telling me, mother, is very wonderful, indeed. I do not think that people feel as thankful as they ought to do, to God, for giving them their arms and hands.

M. That is true, my son, and, after I have explain-

ON NATURAL THEOLOGY.

ed to you some of the parts of the arm and hand; and how they are put together; and how you can move them, only by *thinking to have them move*, you will see still more why you ought to be truly thankful to God, for giving you such a curious and useful instrument. with which to do so many things that are necessary for your happiness and improvement.

You must be very attentive, and patient, or you will not understand me.

R. I will try to be so, mother.

M. You have seen the bones of some animals, my son, have you not?

R. Oh! yes, mother, I have often seen them, when we have had meat at dinner, or turkies and fowls. You know, you sometimes, give me the leg of a fowl, which you call the drumstick; but it looks only a very little like one.

M. Well, there are a great many bones in your arm and hand, and you can feel them, through the flesh, with your hand. On the following page, is a drawing of the bones in your arm and hand.

You see, from the shoulder (a), to the elbow (b), there is only *one bone;* but, from the elbow to the wrist, there are *two bones.*

The bone (c), is called the *shoulder bone.* The bone (d), which joins the wrist, on the side where the thumb is, is called the *radius.* The bone (e), which joins the wrist on the side where the little finger is, is called the *ulna*.

You must remember these names, Robert.

R. I will try, mother: the *shoulder-bone ;*—the *radius ;*—the *ulna*.

M. I shall first explain to you, my son, about the *joint of the arm, at the shoulder*.

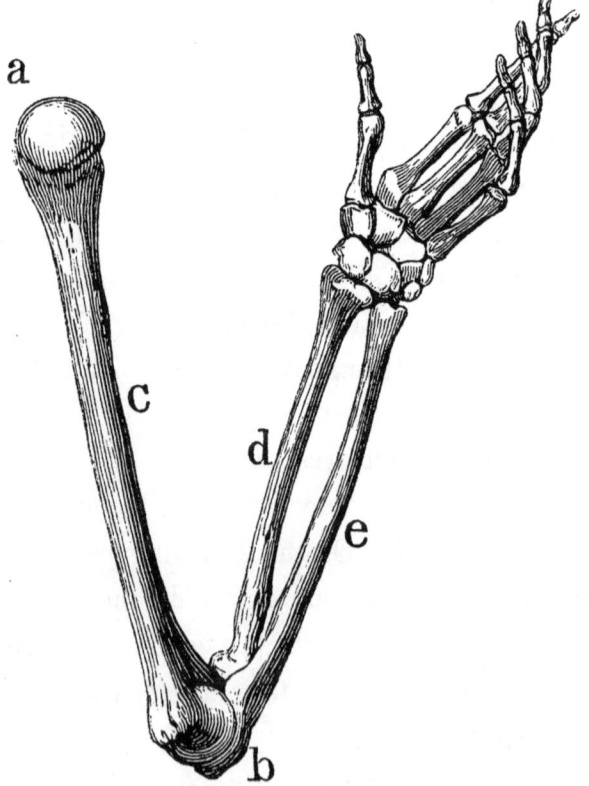

R. What is a *joint*, mother? I know where the joints are; for I have joints in my thumb and fingers, so that I can bend and move them, a great many different ways. But the joint is covered with flesh, and I cannot see it. What is it like?

M. There are different kinds of joints in the body, my son. Some are something like the *hinge to a door*, which may be called *the joint of the door;* by the help of which, the door can be made to open and shut. You see it can move only *one* way, backwards and forwards.

The joints of your fingers, and the joints at your elbows, are *hinge-joints.*

By the help of them, you can shut and open your fingers; and, if your elbow is leaning on a table, you can let your hand go down to the table, and raise it up again, so as to have it touch your shoulder. This joint, like the hinge on the door, can move only one way.

Go, and look at the hinge of the door. You will see, that one part of the hinge, which is fastened on to the door, fits into the other part of the hinge which is fastened on to the door-post, so as to move in it, and thus let the door move. These two parts of the hinge, moving the one in the other, may be called a *joint,* and they are fastened together by an iron pin, or piece of wire.

This iron pin passes through them, up and down, and keeps them together; so that there is no danger of the door's falling down, or getting out of its place.

In the same way, in our bodies, where there are joints, the end of one bone fits on to the end of another bone, and is fastened to it, not with a pin, but by something like very strong, tough threads, or cords; and, by something like a little bag, which goes all round the end of the two bones; so that it helps, with the cords, to keep them firmly together, and they move easily, without any danger of getting out of their place. The ends of the bones do not quite touch each other. The end of each bone is covered with something softer than the bone, but not so soft as flesh. You sometimes see it on the bones of meat, at dinner, and it is called *gristle*. It is very tough, and difficult to be broken, and is a little elastic, something like india-rubber. This gristle keeps the hard bones from jarring and rubbing against each other, which would be very unpleasant. Besides, without this gristle, the bones would not move so easily, and they would be likely to wear away, we use them so constantly and so much.

You see, Robert, that God shows you, in the way in which he has made your arm and hand, his great wisdom, and power, and goodness.

Even *one single joint*, which I have been telling you about, shows the wonderful *design, and contrivance, and skill of God.*

R. It does, indeed, mother.

M. But, my son, there is something about a joint which is yet more wonderful.

R. What is that, mother?

M. What do people have to do to the wheels of their wagons, after they have run some time, and begin to go hard and slow, and make a creaking, unpleasant noise?

R. They have to grease them. And do you not remember, mother, that you put a little sweet oil into the *joint* of my knife, the other day, and how easy it made it open and shut. I could hardly open it before.

M. Well, my son, there is something a little like sweet oil, only a great deal more smooth, which is constantly softening those parts of the joints which move against each other, and making them slippery, so that they move easily and pleasantly.

This *joint-oil is made* inside of the little elastic bag, which, I told you, goes all round the ends of the two bones, at the joint. The bag holds the oil, and keeps it from running out.

If there is disease in the joint, and this oil is not made, the joint becomes stiff, and one bone creaks upon another, and feels very uncomfortable.

Now, God has made our joints so skilfully, and so well, that the joints of most persons go safely and pleasantly all their lives, and never get out of order.

And when we consider that there are about two hundred and fifty bones in our bodies, connected together by various joints; and how often we move the most of these joints, even *in one day;* and how many *millions, and millions, and millions, of times,* an old man has moved them, from the time that he was a little infant,—is it not wonderful, how *long and how well they last!*

What man could make a hinge of a door, or a wheel of a wagon, that would move so often, and wear so long, without having any thing done to it to keep it in order.

We have often to grease the wheels of our wagons, and sometimes to put in new spokes, and get new wheels made; and we have to oil the hinges of our doors, and sometimes the screws work out, and the hinges grow loose, and we have to put them in order, or get new ones.

But we take no care of our joints. We hardly ever think about them. God has made them to *keep on* going well, and, in doing this, what wonderful design, and contrivance, and skill he has shown!

R. Mother, I am sure, that *one joint is enough to make any body believe that there is a* **God**, and that he made our bodies and souls.

M. When you use your joints, then, my son, think

of God, and how he shows himself to you in your curious body which he has made; and how you ought to love him, for having given you such a body; and how you ought to use it, and all its parts, in serving him, and in doing good to others.

But we must stop now. When we talk together again, I will explain to you more particularly about *the joint at the shoulder*, and, afterwards, about the other parts of the arm.

R. Before we go, mother, may I ask you only one question?

M. Do, my son.

R. Was there ever any body who did not believe, that there is a God, who made our joints, and our bodies?

M. There have been a very few persons, my son, who have said, that they did not believe, that there is a God, but that all beings and things were made *by chance*. Such persons are called *atheists*.

R. What do they mean, mother, when they say, that chance made things? What is chance?

M. If you should take two hundred and fifty little wooden blocks, of different sizes and shapes; (just as many as there are bones in our bodies;) and, *without any design*, throw them all together into a heap; and they should, pretty soon, begin to move about, of themselves, and one block go towards some other block, and fit themselves together; and at last, all come in exact order, like the bones in our bodies, and *keep so;*—so that it would be very difficult for you to pull them apart,—then, *all this would happen by chance.*

It might have happened very differently; *but it happened to happen just as it did;* and there was not the least design, or contrivance, or skill, about it.

R. I never could believe *that*, mother, and I do not think, any body else could.

M. Atheists, my son, say they believe so. But they must either be exceedingly wicked, or very foolish, to believe so.

I will tell you more about them, and about chance, which they say made all things, some other time.

DIALOGUE IV.

Mother. I promised, Robert, to explain to you more particularly about *the joint at the shoulder*, and about the other parts of the arm.

Do you wish to have me do it now, or would you rather go and play?

ON NATURAL THEOLOGY. 45

Robert. I had rather talk with you, mother, and learn more of the design, and contrivance, and skill, which God shows me in my curious body that he has made.

M. Well, be attentive, then, and I will begin.

Here is a drawing of the joint at the shoulder, which I wish you to examine.

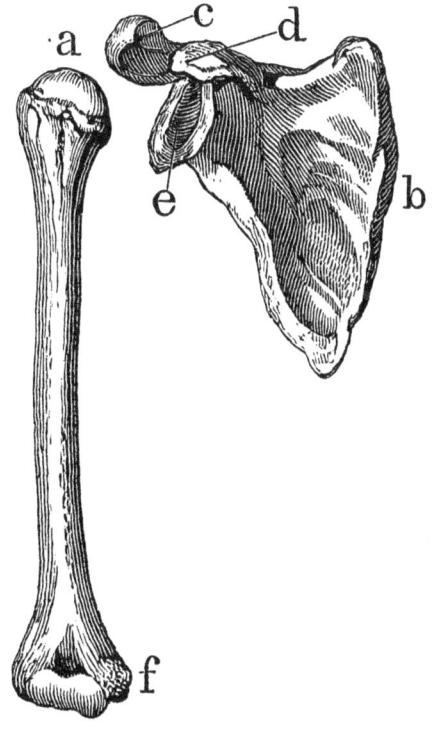

R. Which arm is it, mother?

M. It is the right arm, and only the bones are

drawn. *The gristle* on the ends of the bones; and *the little bag* which goes round them, and helps to keep them together, and holds the joint oil; and the threads or cords that fasten the bones together; about which I told you,———are not drawn. If they had been, you could not have seen the bones so distinctly. I will show you the drawings of them at some other time.

R. Mother, do you call this *a hinge-joint?* It does not seem to me, to look, at all, like a hinge.

M. No, my son, it is not a hinge-joint. It is quite a different kind of joint. If it was a hinge-joint, you would be able to move your arm, at the shoulder, *only one way*, right up and down. A door, you know, can be moved only one way, to open and shut it. The joint at your elbow, is a *hinge-joint*, and you cannot move your arm at the elbow, round and round, as you can at the shoulder.

A hinge-joint at the shoulder, would have been very inconvenient. God knew that it would. He, therefore, made it very different from a hinge-joint; and this shows you, not only his contrivance and skill, but that he had a *particular design*, in making the joint at the shoulder, just as he did.

R. What was his design, mother, in making it so?
M. You will see, by and by, my son.

Look at the upper end (a) of the shoulder bone.

ON NATURAL THEOLOGY. 47

It is round, very much like the little ball that you play with.

Now, look at the bone at which I am pointing (b). It is called, *the shoulder-blade*, because it is flat and thin, something like the blade of a knife. You can feel it, directly behind your shoulder.

You see one end of this bone crooks round, like the bill of a crow (c).

You see, too, that there is another end which crooks round also (d).

Between these *hooks*, as we will call them, you see a small hollow place in the shoulder-blade (e).

Around this hollow place, there is a *ring of gristle*, which, with the hollow place, makes a kind of cup, in which the round end of the shoulder-bone, (a), fits exactly, and moves with great ease.

The end of this bone (a), you recollect, is also covered with gristle; and so is the hollow place in the shoulder-blade (e).

R. I do not see the ring of gristle, mother, nor the gristle on the end of the shoulder-bone, in the picture.

M. They are not drawn, my son, but you can think a little, how they would look. I will show them to you, some time, in a picture.

The round end of the shoulder-bone, in your arm, keeps in the hollow cup about which I have been telling you; and it moves round in the cup, every time that you move your arm. It moves easily, too, because the ring, and coverings of gristle, are so smooth and elastic, and because the joint-oil keeps them slippery.

Only try, and see, how easily and quickly, and in how many different ways you can move your arm, at the shoulder-joint.

(Robert does so).

R. Mother, what do you call the shoulder-joint? You said, it is not a *hinge-joint.*

M. We might call it a cup and ball joint. It is more common, however, to call it a *ball and socket joint.* The socket is the hollow place like a cup, which holds the round end of the bone, and in which it moves.

Make your left hand hollow, as much like a cup as you can; and shut the thumb and fingers of your right hand, as the boys do, when they double up a fist.

Now, put your right hand into your left hand; and hold it fast with the thumb and fingers of the left hand; and move your right hand round as many different ways as you can.

(Robert does so).

R. Mother, I can move it all sorts of ways. I can make my right arm go up and down, or forwards and backwards, or round and round, very quick, indeed.

M. Well, this is something like *the joint at the*

shoulder. The two hooked ends of the shoulder-blade (c d), which you see in the picture, clasp round the round end of the shoulder-bone (a), and help to keep it in its place, somewhat as the thumb and fingers of your left hand did your right hand. But this alone would not be enough to keep the shoulder-bone in its place. Something more is necessary.

R. Mother, *how* is the end of the shoulder-bone kept so strongly in the hollow cup, and never gets out of it?

M. Call it *socket*, my son.

The end of the shoulder-bone is kept in the socket, in this way:

The little bag that holds the joint-oil, and the two hooked ends of the shoulder blade, help to keep the end of the shoulder-bone in the socket; but, besides this, there are strips of hard and strong flesh, and several very tough and strong cords, that are fastened to these strips of flesh, which pass over the shoulder-joint, in various ways, and bind it, and keep it from moving out of the socket.

The strips of flesh, are called *muscles*, and the cords that are fastened to the muscles, are called *tendons*.

The muscles and tendons are fastened to the bones, on different sides of the joints. They pull the bones, and make them move on their joints, a great many different ways. Besides this, they bind the shoulder joint, and keep it in its place, as I have just told you.

R. Mother, do explain to me more about these muscles and tendons. They must be very curious; I wish I could see them.

M. We must not attend to too many things at once, Robert. You can understand things best, by attending to only one at a time.

I intend to tell you more, hereafter, about the muscles and tendons, and to show you some pictures of them.

R. I shall be very glad, mother, and thank you very much.

M. I have done explaining to you, Robert, about the joint at the shoulder.

Now I will tell you about *the joint at the elbow*, which is, also, very curious, and shows you the design, contrivance, and skill of God, in making it.

Here is a drawing of it, which I wish you to examine.

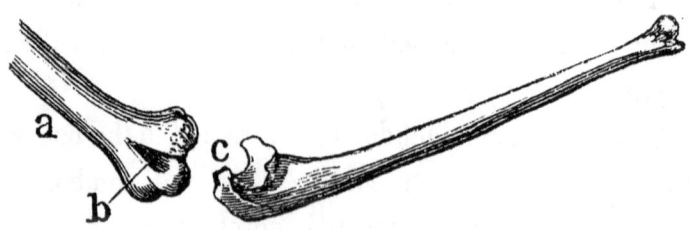

M. It is the right arm which you are looking at, and the elbow is towards you, as if the person were standing with his back to you.

R. That, mother, is a part of the shoulder-bone (a), about which you have been telling me.

M. Yes, but you do not see the round end, which sets into the socket, at the shoulder-joint.

The other end of the bone, which you see, has a very different shape.

There is a hollow place (b), at this end, into which a hooked part (c) of another bone, sets. You recollect, I showed you this bone, (see page 38), and told you that it was called, the *ulna*. It is this bone which moves up and down, at the elbow joint, when the whole arm is stretched out, and the shoulder-bone kept still.

R. I shall remember, mother, to call it the *ulna*. You told me, too, that the ulna, at its lower end, joins the wrist, on the side where the little finger is.

M. Well, a hooked end of the ulna, (c), you see, sets into a hollow place (b) of the shoulder-bone, at the elbow joint. It is this hooked end of the ulna on which you lean, when you say, that you lean on your elbow. You can feel it very easily with your thumb and fingers.

Now, suppose the person, at whose right arm you

are looking, to turn round and face you. You will see the inside of the arm, thus.

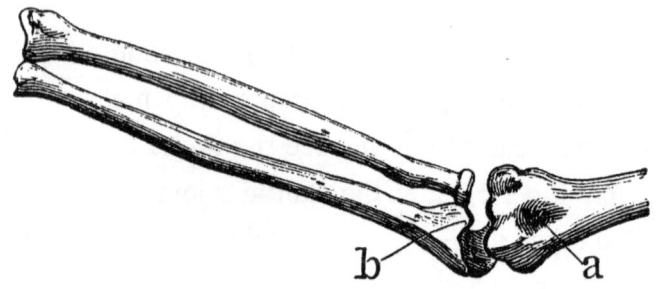

Look at the lower end of the shoulder-bone, and you see a small, hollow place (a), into which another hooked end (b) of the ulna sets. This hollow place, however, is quite shallow, not so deep as the one on the other side, which I showed you; and this end is not so long and hooked as the other end.

These two hooked ends of the ulna, clasp round the end of the shoulder-bone, and form a joint, which is called a hinge-joint, so that you can move your arm, at the elbow; but you can move it only one way.

When you straighten your arm, the hooked end, on the outside, goes into the hollow place on the outside, and sets firm and fast into it, and helps to keep the ulna in its place, and from going any farther back.

When you bend your arm, so as to bring your hand up to your shoulder, the crooked end of the ulna on the inside, goes into the hollow place on the inside, and helps keep the ulna in its place, and from going any farther that way.

R. Mother, I wish I could see the real bones, and then I should know exactly how they look.

M. When you grow older, my son, perhaps you may see them; but I think you can understand about them, pretty well, from looking at the pictures.

R. I do not know, mother, that I understand exactly, how the two hooked ends of the ulna, going quite down into the two hollow places, in the end of the shoulder-bone, help to keep the arm from going too far, one way or the other.

M. I think I can explain it to you a little further, so that you will understand it.

Shut up your left hand tight, as the boys do, when they double up a fist.

Now crook the thumb and fore-finger of your right hand, so as to make half the letter O, and shut up the three other fingers.

Clasp your left hand with the thumb and fore-finger of your right hand; so that the fore-finger may lie between the lower joint of the little finger, and of the finger next to it; and that the thumb may lie just under the thumb of the left hand.

Roll your right hand on your left hand, *from you, and towards you*, keeping it as close as you can to your left hand, and making the fore-finger and thumb of your right hand as hooked as you can.

You will see, that, after your right hand has moved

a little one way or the other, it will stop; and if there were two, small, hollow places, in your left hand, in which the ends of your thumb and finger could set, this would help still more to keep your right hand from moving any farther, and to keep it in its place

The middle joint of the fore-finger of your right hand, represents, or is like the elbow of your arm; and the clasping of the fore-finger and thumb round your left hand, is something like the *hinge joint at the elbow.*

R. Now, mother, I seem to understand it better. But you have not told me any thing, yet, about the radius.

M. One thing at a time, my son. Just now, you did not quite understand about the motion of the ulna round the end of the shoulder-bone. Be attentive, and not in a hurry. Be sure, that you understand every thing as I am explaining it to you; and, if you do not understand it, tell me so, and ask me all the questions that you wish to do.

That is the way, that little boys and girls should do, and big men and women, too, when they are learning any thing new and difficult.

If people would all do so, they would know a great deal more than they do; they would not so often be mistaken; and they would be a great deal wiser.

This evening I will tell you about the radius; and

ON NATURAL THEOLOGY. 55

then, you can ask me any more questions that you choose, about what I have already told you.

DIALOGUE V.

ROBERT. Mother, it is more than an hour yet, before I must go to bed. Remember, you promised to tell me about the radius.

MOTHER. Well, my son, I always mean to keep my promises. Come, sit down by the table, and look at this drawing.

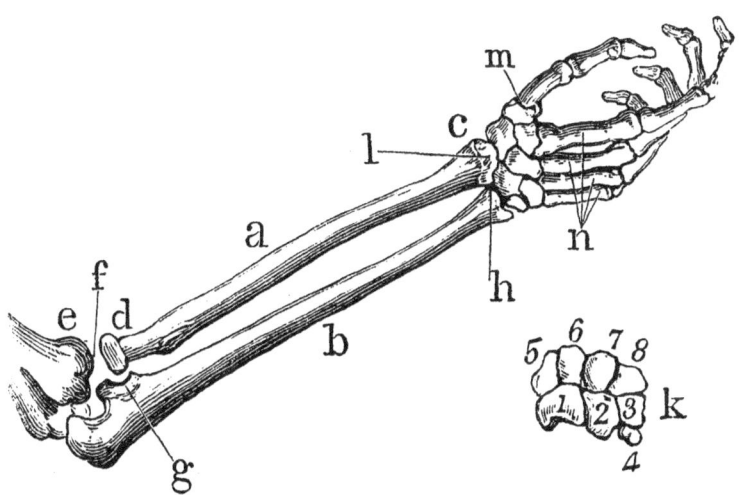

R. Oh! mother, I remember which the *radius* is. There it is (a), just above the ulna (b).

M. You are right, Robert. You see, one end (c) of it, is on that side of the hand where the thumb is, and the other end (d) almost touches the lower end (e) of the shoulder bone.

R. Does it not set in to the shoulder bone, mother as the hooked ends of the ulna do?

M. No, my son, but there is a small, round knob (f), on the end of the shoulder bone, on which the end of the radius moves. The end of the radius is made to fit on to this knob; so that it is a very little like a *ball and socket joint*.

The radius moves two ways, on this knob;—up and down, when the elbow joint moves, and the hand is moved up and down;—and it turns round on this knob, when the hand is turned round, at the wrist.

R. Mother, how many curious motions, the different bones have!

M. Yes, my son. Do you think, that you could cut out some little sticks of wood; and shape them; and fit them together; so as to make them have as many different, curious motions, as the bones of the arm have?

R. No, mother, I should not have contrivance and skill enough.

M. Well, my son, as we go on in our explanation, you will keep seeing more and more of the wonderful design, and contrivance, and skill of God, and of his goodness too, in making for you such a curious and convenient instrument as the arm and hand.

R. Mother, the end of the radius (d), next to the shoulder bone, looks like a button.

M. Yes, my son, and it is called a *button-head*. You see the edge of it just touches the upper side of the ulna.

R. Is it fastened to it, mother?

M. No, my son. If it were, you could not turn your hand round, at the wrist.

R. Why not, mother? I do not understand that.

M. One end of the radius (c), Robert, is fastened to some little bones, which are at the bottom of that side of the hand where the thumb is. To these little bones, the hand is fastened; and it rests, and moves, on them.

Now when you keep your arm quite still, so as not to move it either at the shoulder, or at the elbow, and turn your hand over, and back again, the little bones at the bottom of the hand, must turn over, too.

These little bones are fastened to the radius; so that the radius must turn round also. And this it could not do, if its *button-head* (d) were fastened tight to the ulna. If it were, the radius could only move up and down, and only when the ulna did, for, being fastened tight to it, the radius would move just as the ulna does.

Do you understand me?

R. I think I do, mother, but I wish to look at the drawing, a little more.

M. Just as long as you please, Robert.

R. Mother, it seems to me, that when the radius turns round, at the same time that the hand does, at the wrist,—that *the edge of the button-head* (d) must roll on the side of the ulna.

M. You are right, my son. It does; and there is a small, hollow place (g) scooped out of the upper side of the end of the ulna, in which the edge of the button head fits exactly, and in which it rolls, whenever it turns round.

It is this turning round of the radius, that enables you to turn your hand round, at the wrist, so that you can hold the back of it upwards, and then the palm of it upwards, just as you choose.

R. Is the end of the radius at the wrist (c), fastened to the ulna, mother?

M. No, my son, for then the radius could not turn round. It could only move as the ulna does.

But, at the wrist, it is the ulna that has a sort of button-head (h), and the hollow place which fits it, is scooped out of the radius; so that, when the radius turns round, this hollow place rolls on the button-head of the ulna.

And God has made all this so exactly, and so curiously, to enable you, both to bend your arm at the elbow, and, at the same time, to turn your hand round, whenever you wish to do it.

Put your two fore-fingers close along side of each other. Keep them close at the lower joint, while you roll the fore-finger of the right hand over, and across, the fore-finger of the left hand, and back again.

(Robert does so.)

Well, this is something like the rolling of the radius over, and across, the ulna, when you turn your hand over, and back again. And you see the reason, why, at the elbow, the button-head of the radius *rolls in* the hollow place (g) of the ulna,—and why, at the wrist, the hollow place of the radius *rolls on* the button-head (h) of the ulna.

In this way, the end of the radius, at the wrist, has more motion than the end, at the elbow. It has a larger sweep, and the hand can be turned over farther, and more easily

R. Curious! curious! Mother, are all the other parts of the body as curious?

M. Yes, my son, and many of them are a great deal more so.

R. I should think, it would take a great while to understand about them all.

M. It would so, Robert; a great many books have been written about them, by very wise and learned men. And yet, *all is not known about them.* Probably, many more curious, and wonderful, things will yet be found out. Then we shall have still more reason to admire, and be thankful for, the great wisdom and power, and skill, and goodness of God, in the bodies which he has made for our souls to live in, and to use, in so many ways, for our happiness, and for that of our fellow men.

But we must talk a little more about the *elbow-joint* before you go to bed. Are you tired?

R. Not at all, mother; I could sit here an hour longer, what you say is so entertaining and instructive to me.

M. I only wish to tell you, how the shoulder-bone, the ulna, and the radius, are fastened together, at the elbow-joint. For there are some things about it, a little different from the joint at the shoulder, and which show still further the design, contrivance, and skill of God.

The ends of the bones, as at the shoulder-joint, are covered with *gristle*, the use of which I explained to you. The *joint-oil*, too, is furnished, and kept in a bag which surrounds the joint; and you recollect what it is for.

Several muscles, also, and tendons, (the strips of hard flesh, and tough, strong cords, about which I told you), pass across the joint, and being fastened, above and below it, to help keep the ulna and the radius in their places.

But there is still something more done, to keep them in their places; and this was very necessary, for there is a great strain at the elbow-joint, when we lift any thing very heavy, or do any thing very hard, with our hands.

Here is a drawing, at which I wish you to look very attentively, while I am explaining it to you.

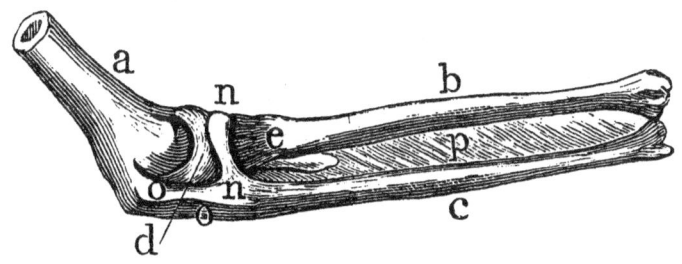

(a) is the shoulder-bone, (b) the radius, and (c) the ulna, of the left arm.

They are all bound together by the bag of the joint (d), which is not very strong itself, but is made so, by some ligaments that cross it in different directions.

R. Mother, what is a *ligament*?

M. I was just going to tell you; but I am glad that you asked me, for it shows that you recollect what I have told you—always to ask the meaning of any words that you do not understand.

If you should wind the end of your handkerchief round two of your fingers, so as to bind them together, it would be called a *ligament*.

A ligament is a band of any kind, put round two or more things, to bind them together.

The ligaments, in our bodies, are either flat, like a piece of tape, or round, like a cord. They are very tough and strong, and are made up of a great many, very fine threads, very close together—closer than a strong man could twist a great many, fine, strong cords together.

Now, look again at the drawing. The ligament (e), is a part of the bag, and goes over the button-head of the radius. It is very hard, and something like gristle. It is strengthened very much, by another ligament (n n,) which, you see, goes across the bag.

There are, also, two ligaments (o o), which are small, but strong slips, that go from the end of the shoulder-bone, to the bottom of the large hook of the ulna.

Then, there is a ligament (p), passing between the radius and the ulna.

So you see what care is taken, to make the elbow-joint firm and strong, and to keep all the bones in their places, while they can still move so curiously, *around, and upon, and across, each other.*

You understand now, I suppose, enough about the joints, at the shoulder, and at the elbow, to see the *design* which God had in making them as he did.

R. I do, pretty well, mother. His design was, to have them move, in the best way for our using them.

M. That is right, Robert. And only think, if the *hinge joint* was at the shoulder, and the *ball and socket joint* at the elbow, how awkwardly we should move our arm.

It would be difficult then, and, indeed, impossible for us, to do many things with our arms and hands, which we now do with great ease and quickness.

Could any body suppose, that the man who *first thought* of making a pencil-case, like my silver one, had not a *particular design* in making it? When you examine it, and see how all its parts are curiously made, and skilfully put together, do you not think, at once, and believe, that a man made it, and that he had a *particular design* in making all its parts, and in putting them together, just as he did?

And when you examine the hinge of a door, can you believe, that it was made for *any other purpose,* than to have the door swing upon it? Did not the man *who first thought* how to make it, have a *parti-*

cular design in making all its parts, and in putting them together, just as he did?

What else could the pencil-case have been made for, than to hold a small, new kind of lead pencil, different from the old kind, and more convenient for a person to write with?

What else could the hinge of a door have been made for, than to have the door swing upon it, and open and shut?

In the same way, *what else* could the joints at the shoulder and elbow, have been made for, than to help the arm and hand to move, easily and quickly, a great many different ways, so that we can use them for doing a great many different things?

And why were the shoulder-joint, and the elbow-joint, made so differently from each other? Here, we see another *particular design*. For, if there were no such design, they would have been made alike, just as the two hinges of a door are.

There is no reason why the two hinges of a door should be *unlike*. No, there are good reasons why they should be made *exactly alike*.

Now, there are no good reasons why the shoulder and elbow joints should be made alike. If they were made so, they would be very awkward and inconvenient, and quite useless for doing many things which we now do easily and well.

But you can see many good reasons, why they should be made unlike, and why, at the shoulder, there should be a *ball and socket joint*, and, at the elbow, a *hinge joint*.

In making them so, God had a *particular design;* and, when we examine their curious parts, we not only believe that there is a God who made them, but that *he made all the parts, and put them together, just as he did, for one purpose, and for no other.*

Every time that we move our arms and our hands, or do any thing with them, shows us *this one purpose* for which God made *the joints* exactly as he has made them.

R. Mother, how little men know, and how little they can do! How wise, and powerful, and skilful, God is!

M. Remember, too, my son, *how good God is!* He is good in making all the parts of your body, just as he has made them; and in keeping them in order, as he does; and in giving you health and strength; and in keeping you safe from danger, so that none of your limbs have been broken, or any part of your body injured.

Has not God a right to command you, never to use your arms and hands for doing any thing wrong, nor your lips and tongue for saying any thing wrong, but to use them, and your whole body, in obeying and serving him, and in doing good to others?

R. Yes, indeed, I think he has, mother.

M. Remember it, my son; and always fear to use your body for any wrong purpose, and thus sin against God. For God looks on all who sin against him, with very great displeasure.

R. I hope, mother, that I shall always remember what you have told me, and try to use my arms, and hands, and lips, and tongue, and all the parts of my body, just as I ought to do, and to do good with them.

M. I hope you will, my son, and that God will enable you to do so.

DIALOGUE VI.

Mother. You have been a good boy, Robert, and said your lessons well, and now I will explain to you something more about the arm and hand.

Robert. I shall be very much obliged to you, mother, for doing it. For I should not like to stop now, and not know any thing about the wrist and hand, since I understand pretty well about the bones and joints in the arm.

M. You will see, my son, that the bones and joints in the arm, are all connected with the bones and joints of the wrist and hand; indeed, they were designed principally to enable you to use your hand. The different kinds of motions, at the shoulder and elbow-joints, enable you to carry your hand from one place to another; to reach up high, or down low, and get any thing; to stretch your hand forward, or to put it behind you; and to move it, in one direction and another, as you may wish.

So you see all the parts of your arm and hand, are only parts of one and the same instrument, made, and put together, with *one design*, to enable you to use it easily and quickly, for your own good, and the good of others.

R. Mother, God must have thought a good deal, *how* to make the arm and hand.

It would take a man a great while to think how to make such a curious and useful instrument, and one, too, that should always keep in good order.

M. My son, *God's thoughts are not as our thoughts.*

When we say that God designs and contrives, we do not mean, that he does so as we do.

We have to *think long and hard*, in designing any thing which it is difficult to make. Some men have spent many years in doing this. *The man that first designed a steamboat, did;* and yet he did not make it as good as it might have been made. Other persons have since designed and made steamboats, and made them better in many things. And other persons will probably make steamboats, still better, more safe, and more useful, and thus show *their design and contrivance.*

But God thinks immediately, and without the least difficulty, how to make the things which he wishes to make, and which appear to us the most difficult to be made.

He knows all things, and therefore, knows all the different ways in which things can be made, and how their parts can be put together, and *what is the best way of doing this.*

When a man designs and contrives any thing, he could not do it, if he had not learned a great many things from others.

You could not design and contrive how to make a new kind of kite, if you had not seen the boys make kites, and thus learned yourself how to make them.

But God learns nothing from other beings. He knows, and has always known how all kinds of beings and things can be made, and for what they can be made; and he can make them whenever he chooses, exactly and perfectly, as easily and quickly as you can speak a word.

R. What do you mean, mother, when you say that *God is skilful?*

M. Do you remember, that you told me, some days ago, what skill is?

R. Yes, mother.

M. Well, tell me again, what it is.

R. It is—after any body has contrived how to make any thing—to get every thing ready, and put all the parts together, just as they ought to be, so as to have the thing well made, and to do all this easily, and exactly, without making any mistake.

M. We do not get our skill at once. It takes us a long time to get it. You had to make a good many kites, *before you were skilful in making one.* Little children are not skilful. They make a great many mistakes, when they try to make any thing. They must grow older, and often see other persons do things, and have things explained to them, and think a great deal, and use their hands a great deal, before they can have skill in making, or doing things.

But God does not get his skill in this way. He never has to learn, how to make or to do any thing. His skill is perfect.

By this, I mean, that he never makes the smallest mistake in making any thing, and that he can make it at once, and without the least difficulty, exactly as it is best it should be made.

When the most skilful man makes any thing, other persons will, sometimes, see some way in which it might be made a little better.

Nobody can see any way in which the things which God has made, could be made at all better.

The arm and hand, with all their joints and parts, could not be made better in any one thing, when we consider the being for whom they were made; the body to which they belong; and the uses for which they were designed. Can any body point out a way, in which any part of the arm or hand could be made better? Nobody can. In them God shows us his perfect skill; and *in all things which God has made, his skill is perfect.*

This is some explanation of the skill of God. But all that we know, or all that we can think about it, is far, very far below what it truly is.

The skill of God is one part of his wisdom; and he is wise in knowing every thing, which it is best should be done, or made; and also, in knowing the very best way in which it should be done, or made.

The wisdom of God is as much greater than our wisdom, as this world is greater than one grain of sand; yes, as millions, and millions, and millions, of this world, would be greater than one such grain; and as many more worlds, added to these, as all the people that ever lived could count, if they should do nothing but count all their lives.

The wisdom of God is infinite. But come, look at this drawing, and I will explain to you about the wrist and hand. (See page 55.)

The wrist is made up of eight small bones (k), which you see are of different sizes and shapes.

They are tied together very strongly by bands, or ligaments, that go across them, and they make a sort of ball, on which the other bones of the hand move. You see, there are two rows of these eight bones. Two in the lower row (1, 2), are so put together, that they form a ball, which fits into a hollow place, or socket, (1), *in the end of the radius*, and forms the wrist-joint.

This joint at the wrist is very moveable. It is also very strong; for it is almost like a hinge-joint, the hollow of the radius, and the ball of the bone that fits into it, both being very long. It has a very free motion, too, for it turns with the radius, whenever the radius turns.

The other two small bones, in the lower row, (3, 4), are connected with the end of the ulna; but they do not make an exact joint with it. They roll upon it, and make the motions of the hand, at the wrist-joint, easier.

R. There are four bones, mother, in the upper row.

M. Yes, and the one (5) next to the thumb. is a pretty large one. It has a socket in which the ball of the thumb moves. The second bone from this (7) has a long, round head, which is jointed with the hollow of the bone below (2); so that it makes a sort of ball and socket-joint, by which the upper row of bones, moves upon the lower row.

All these eight bones, in the two rows, where they are joined to each other, are covered with smooth gristle (or cartilage, as it is also called.) This, you know, makes them move easily. They are bound firmly togethe , by a great many cross ligaments of different kinds, and they make something like *one great joint*, but much more *flexible* than a single joint would be.

R. Mother, what does flexible mean ?

M. Can you bend this andiron ?

R. I cannot, but I can bend the handle of that little whip that lies on the floor.

M. The handle of the whip is flexible, Robert, but the andiron is not. The joints of your fore-finger, make it very flexible. See, in how many different ways, you can bend it.

A blade of grass, too, is very flexible. An icicle is

not flexible. If you try to bend it, it immediately breaks in two.

R. I think, there is no part of my body, mother, which is so flexible as my hand and fingers.

M. You see *the design* of God, my son, in making them so. Ten thousand, thousand, different things, which men and women learn to do, so curiously, so quickly, and so easily, with their hands and fingers, could not be done, if there were not so many joints, and bones, moving smoothly on each other, and thus making the hands and fingers very flexible.

Look at the picture, again, Robert. Above the upper row of the eight bones, about which I have been telling you, you see five long bones.

The bone under the thumb, has a large, round head, which forms a ball and socket joint (m) with the bone below it, about which I told you.

This gives the thumb a very wide and free motion, which, as you may see, from using it, with your fingers, it was very necessary that it should have.

The other four bones (n), with which the fingers are jointed, have flat and square heads, which set very firmly upon the upper row of the eight bones of the wrist. They are bound to these bones by ligaments, and move but little upon them.

The thumb, you see, has but two bones, unless you count the lower bone with a round head, which, perhaps, ought to be done; and then the thumb will have three bones, and three joints, just as the fingers have.

The two upper joints of the thumb and fingers, are hinge-joints; and these joints are made very strong, by ligaments on each side of them.

With the help of these joints, we can bend and crook the thumb and fingers so as to take hold of, or grasp, any thing very firmly. And we can do this so much the easier, and better, because the thumb stands out from the fingers, on one side, and is opposite to them.

You know, how exactly you can put your thumb and fingers round your ball, so as to hold it very tight.

How well, too, you can take hold of a rope, and pull it, with your two hands.

And, it would seem, as if the thumb, and the two fingers next to it were made on purpose to write with, and to sew with. What nice motions we can make with them, and what very fine things we can take hold of, and pick up with them.

R. The nails help a good deal, mother, in doing that; and so they do, in untying hard knots.

M. That is true, my son; the nails, also, are a very curious and useful part of the hand.

But, I have a little more to tell you about the joints of the fingers.

The lower joints of the fingers, which we call the knuckles, are ball and socket joints. The hollow place is on the lower part of the finger bones, which move on the round heads of the bones below them (n). These joints give the fingers very free and easy motions, and enable us to separate them from each other, and to spread them out, like a fan.

If the middle joints of the thumb and fingers were ball and socket joints, we could not take hold of things, and clasp around them, so firmly with our thumb and fingers as we now do.

They would be as awkward and inconvenient, as, I told you, a ball and socket joint at the elbow, would be.

R. Mother, the hand is most curious and wonderful, indeed! I never thought, before, that it had so many different parts, put together, just as they are.

M. And yet, my son, I have not told you about many other parts of the arm and hand, quite as curious and wonderful.

I have only told you about the bones, and joints, and some of the ligaments.

But from *these alone*, you see, with how much skill and goodness God has made the arm and hand for your use and comfort. Did you ever think, *how many things* you can do with your arms and hands, although you are but a little boy?

R. I know, I can do a great many things with

them, mother. But I can do one thing with my fingers, that I have never told you about.

M. What is that?

R. I can make the alphabet that the deaf and dumb use. A little boy taught it to me last Saturday afternoon. Here is an engraving of it, which he gave me.

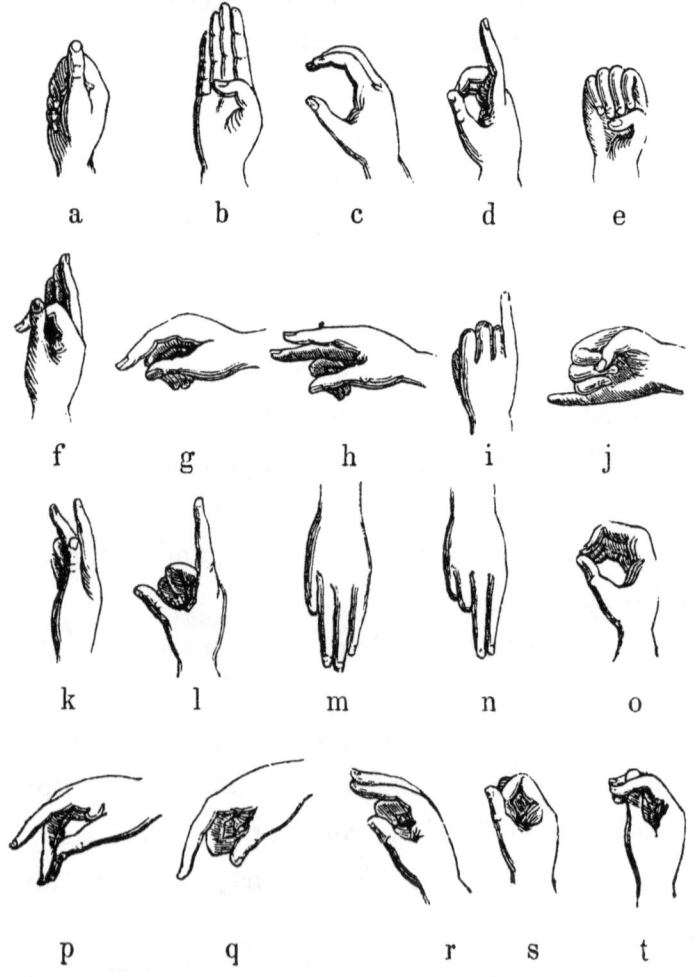

ON NATURAL THEOLOGY. 77

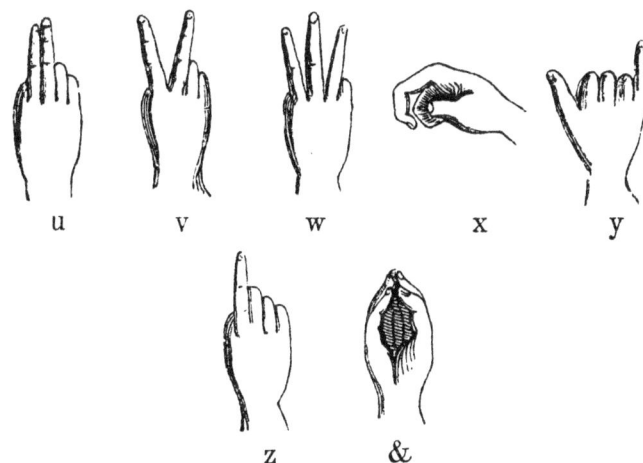

u   v   w   x   y

z   &

[j is made by raising the little finger, and then describing with it, in the air, a curve line, resembling the tail of the j. z is made by raising the fore-finger, and describing with it, in the air, the shape of z. No regard is had to syllables, in spelling words; the end of a word is denoted by a horizontal motion of the hand.]

M. That is another way in which the hand shows the skill and goodness of God.

What would the deaf and dumb do, if they could not talk on their fingers. It is curious to see with what astonishing quickness they can make all the bones and joints of their hands move, when they spell words.

They can spell words four times faster than the best writer can write them on paper with a pen.

R. Mother, what is it that makes the bones move on the joints? The door does not move on its hinges, unless you pull it open, or push it back again.

M I will tell you something about that, my son, to-morrow evening.

Remember what I have already taught you; and if you should find that you have forgotten any thing, I will tell you about it again.

Little boys and girls should not only endeavor to *understand* what is taught them, but to *remember* it, too.

DIALOGUE VII.

Robert. Now, mother, please to explain to me, what it is that makes the bones move on the joints.

Mother. I will, my son; and you must continue to be attentive, and not think about any thing, only what we are talking about.

Tie the end of this handkerchief to the knob of that door, and open the door a very little. Then stand as far as you can from the door, and hold the other end of the handkerchief in your hand.

(Robert does so.)

I have, mother, now what shall I do?

M. Pull the handkerchief.

ON NATURAL THEOLOGY. 79

R. I have, and the door opens further.

M. You see, too, Robert, how it turns on its hinges.

R. I do, mother.

M. Now, shut the door again, but not so as to latch it. Tie the loose end of the handkerchief to the top of this chair on which I am sitting.

Now, put your hand on the middle of the handkerchief, and press it gently down towards the floor.

R. Mother, the door opens just as it did before.

M. Shut it again, without latching it.

Now, take hold of the handkerchief, near the

middle, with both your hands, and let your hands be a few inches apart.

R. I have done so, mother.

M. Bring your hands together, so that they may touch each other.

R. I have, and again the door opens.

M. Well, you see, this last time, how the handkerchief pulled the door open, because it was made shorter, by your bringing your hands together. One end of it was fastened tight to the chair, and this end did not move, because the chair was firm in its place. But the other end was drawn towards the middle of the handkerchief, and drew the door open with it, because the door was not latched, but could be made to move easily on its hinges.

R. I understand all this, very well, mother, but how does it explain the motions of the bones on the joints?

M. Have a little patience, my son, and you will soon see.

Hand me the handkerchief. I am going to tie one end of it round my neck; and do you tie the other round my wrist.

(Mrs. Stanhope and Robert do this.)

Now, Robert, take hold of the middle of the handkerchief, with both your hands, as you did before.

Put them a little ways apart, and, then, bring them together.

R. It raises your hand up, mother, just as before, it pulled the door open.

M. Have you ever seen any thing shrink, Robert?

R. Yes, mother; you know when my mittens were wet, last winter, and I put them near the fire, to dry, they shrunk so much that I could hardly get them on.

M. Well, if there were any way of making the *handkerchief shrink in the middle*, without any body's touching it, it would raise my hand up,— would it not?

R. Yes, I see it would, just as it did, when I brought my hands together.

M. There is something very much like this, Robert,—a kind of fleshy string, in your arm, that shrinks and pulls your hand up, every time that you think to raise it, and bend your arm at the elbow. This string is fastened to one bone above your elbow, and to another bone below it.

R. What is it made of, mother?

M. Do you see the fine, silken threads in my handkerchief?

R. Yes, mother; how many of them there are, and how close they are together.

M. If you should pull out some of these silken

threads, and split each one of them into a great many finer threads, a hundred times finer than the finest hair in your head, would they not be very fine?

R. Oh! yes, mother, very fine, indeed,—and so fine, I do not think I could see them at all.

M. You might see them, however, by looking at them, through the microscope which I showed you the other day.

R. That instrument, mother, that had so many curious glasses in it?

M. Yes, my son, and you recollect you looked through it, at a single hair.

R. I remember mother. The hair looked as large as a small cord.

M. Well, you might see the very fine threads, in the same way; for the microscope would magnify them,—that is, make them look a great deal larger than they really were.

R. But a little, fine thread, like these, mother, would not be strong enough to draw my hand up!

M. A little patience, Robert. I have a good deal to explain to you, yet.

Suppose, one of these very fine threads had wrapped all round it, something very thin, fine, and soft, making a kind of case, or sheath, for it.

R. Mother, nobody could see to do that, unless

they had eyes like microscopes; and, then, the thumb and fingers, even of a little infant, would be too large and clumsy, to take hold of such fine things.

M. Well, you know, you can suppose, that it might be done; or, at least, that God could make it so.

R. Oh! yes, mother, for he can make, or do, any thing that he chooses.

M. Well, my son, *God has made such very small, fine threads*, and such sheaths for them, as I have been telling you about, and they are in your arm, and millions, and millions, and millions of them, are in the different parts of your body.

R. But they are not made of silk, mother.

M. No, Robert, they are made of the same thing that your flesh is made of.

A great many of these very small, fine threads, with their sheaths round them, are laid right along side of each other, so close, that it would be exceedingly difficult to separate them with the finest, sharpest, pen-knife,—and, then, there is one, larger case, that goes around them; keeping them very tight together, and making a sort of small bundle of them.

R. Mother, I should think, they would often get broken, they are so very small and fine.

M. No, my son, God has made them so curiously, and put them together with so much care and skill, that hundreds and thousands of people, who live to be very old, never have a single one of these small, fine threads, broken.

R. Mother, this, I think, is the most wonderful thing that you have told me about, yet.

M. It is, indeed, very wonderful, Robert; but our bodies are all full of wonders. *We are fearfully, and wonderfully made.*

But I have something still more curious to tell you about these small, fine threads, and the little bundles into which they are made.

Several of these little bundles of threads, are laid right along side of each other, or on the top of each other, so as to make a little larger bundle. This bundle, also, has a sheath, or case, round it.

Then, again, several of these larger bundles are put together in the same way, making a still larger bundle, with its sheath all round it.

Sometimes more, and sometimes fewer, of these bundles, are thus put together, till they make one great bundle.

This largest bundle of all, made up of the smaller ones, is called a muscle, and this, also, has a case, or sheath, round it.

By putting so many of these very small, fine threads so closely together in their cases, and bundles, you see that a very strong muscle is made.—a great deal stronger to pull with than my handkerchief is.

R. And is it such a muscle, mother, that pulls my hand up, when I raise it?

M. Yes, my son; and every motion that you can make, in all the different parts of your body, when you speak, or eat, or turn your eyes and head, or sit down, or get up, or walk, or run, or hop, or jump, or climb, or take any thing, or carry any thing, or do any thing; every motion that all the people make, in all their different kinds of business; every motion that all the beasts, and birds, and fishes make; *all these motions are made by the help of muscles.*

R. Mother, I should like to see a muscle very much.

M. You can feel one, Robert, very easily.

Take hold of the inside of your arm, between the elbow and shoulder, and squeeze it, with your thumb and fingers.

R. That is my flesh, mother. It is not hard, like a bone, but quite soft.

M. Well, it is the same thing as a muscle; you feel *the muscle,* or bundle that is made up of the smaller, and still smaller bundles of fine threads, with their cases inside of each other.

Look at this drawing, and you will see some of the muscles, in the arm and hand.

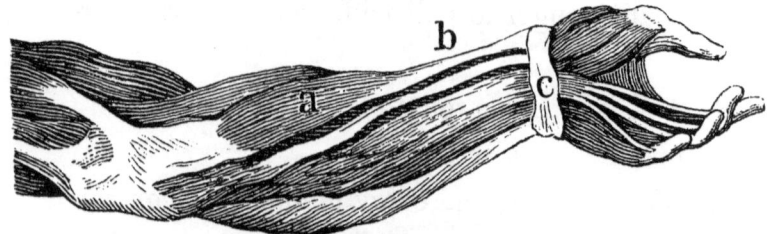

Look at this muscle (a). It is on the inside of the arm. It is fastened, near the elbow, to a knob of bone, on the inside of the shoulder-bone.

You see, it goes along, down the arm, towards the wrist. It grows narrower, and narrower, till it looks like a cord (b).

This part, like a cord, is not a muscle. It is made up of a great many small, fine threads, but they are so made and put together, that the cord which is made out of them, is very different from a muscle.

This cord is called a tendon.

The tendons do not contract, or *shrink*, as the muscles do. They are much harder and firmer than the muscles are. They are very tough and strong, and very hard to be broken.

This tendon (b) looks like a part of the muscle, and as if it grew out of it. But it does not. It is fastened, however, very tight to the muscles, and moves whenever the muscle does.

This tendon, you see, goes quite down to the wrist.

At the wrist, it is fastened, on the inside of the hand, to the bone that lies directly under the lowest bone of the fore-finger.

The muscle and the tendon, which are firmly joined together, you see make one string, the two ends of which are fastened tight to two bones. These bones have the joint at the wrist between them,—the joint at the end of the radius, which I explained to you.

As soon, then, as the muscle (a) *contracts*, it pulls the tendon (b) towards the muscle. The tendon pulls the bone under the fore-finger, the same way; and so the hand bends at the wrist-joint, towards the inside of the arm.

R. But, mother, when you tied one end of the handkerchief round your neck and the other round your wrist, to show me, how the arm moved at the elbow-joint, the handkerchief went straight from the wrist to your neck.

M. I know that, my son. The muscles and tendons do not do so. If they did, they would be outside of the arm.

R. That would look very bad, mother.

M. Yes, and it would be very inconvenient, too.

God has shown us his great wisdom and goodness, in the way in which he has put together the muscles and tendons, and bones and joints. There are no less than forty-three muscles, with their tendons, and thirty bones in the arm and hand; besides ligaments, and many other parts about which I have not had time to tell you. Yet all these are *packed* very close together, within a small space, and covered with the skin, so that we do not see them, and we cannot touch them.

They are packed closer a great deal than you have seen me pack my clothes in a trunk. But they do not get tangled with each other, nor rub against each other, so as to do any harm; nor disturb each other, while they are moving a great many different ways.

Who could have done this, but He who has infinite skill, and power, and goodness! God alone, the maker and preserver of all things, could have done it!

But, before we stop, I wish to explain one thing to you. To do it, I will tie one end of my handkerchief to the fore-finger of your left hand, with the knot on the inside.

(Mrs. Stanhope does so.)

Now, Robert, pull the handkerchief towards your elbow, on the inside of your arm, keeping the handkerchief close to the arm.

R. Mother, as soon as the wrist bends, the handkerchief begins to rise from the arm; and when the wrist is bent as much as it can be, the handkerchief is a good way from the arm.

M. Just so, my son, the tendon, (b) would spring up, if there were not a ligament, (or band), at the wrist, to keep it down. You see this ligament (c), and the tendon (b) goes under it.

R. Is it not harder, mother, to bend the wrist, than if there were no ligament there, and the tendon were pulled straight from the hand to the elbow?

M. Yes, my son; but the muscle is a very strong one, and can pull hard enough. And you know how awkward and inconvenient it would be, to have the muscle and tendon outside of the arm.

But, give me your own handkerchief, and let me tie it round your wrist. Then, my handkerchief and yours will be just like the tendon and band.

(Mrs. Stanhope does so.)

Now pull my handkerchief, Robert, just as you did before.

R. It raises the hand, mother, and bends the wrist very well; but I have to pull harder.

M. Very few of the muscles, my son, pull straight. They and their tendons go under ligaments, and under and across, and around other muscles and tendons, and pull a great many different ways. But they have great power, and can pull as hard as is necessary. If it were not so, how could so many of them be put together into your little body, so as to make so many different kinds of motions.

There are five hundred and twenty-seven muscles in your body; and every time that you breathe, one hundred of these muscles are moved.

R. Mother, I am very much afraid, some of them will get broken, or go wrong.

M. Why so, my son? God, who had the skill and power to make them, and put them together, did it so perfectly, that they get broken, or go wrong, very, very seldom indeed; and then, only when some accident happens to us, or when we have some disease.

You need not be afraid to run, hop, and jump, just as you have always done. That was *one thing* for which your muscles were made. And you should be truly thankful to God, that you can move your limbs so quickly and easily, and play so briskly and happily.

You must soon begin, also, as your muscles grow stronger, to use them in *some kind of work*.

This is *another thing* that they were made for.

God gave them to us, that we might be industrious. You must learn to be industrious, and to work with your hands.

This is the sure way to have a sound, healthy, and strong body, and a cheerful and active mind. Besides, you do not know how poor you may be, so that you will be obliged to work, to earn money to buy clothes and food, and to take care of yourself.

Little boys that grow up, without learning at all, to work with their hands, although they may learn a great deal in books, often become quite sick and weak, when they are men, and so cannot use their knowledge for any good purpose. And, sometimes, they cannot get any body to do any thing for them, and they are helpless, like little infants, and do not know how to do any thing for themselves, and suffer a great deal. And, sometimes, they become poor, and cannot earn any money, which they might very soon do, if they knew how to labor with their hands.

R. Mother, you know, I love to carry in wood for the parlor fire, and I will carry it a great deal more, when I grow older, and saw and split it, too.

M. That is right, my son. Be industrious, and that will keep you from evil, and be one of the surest ways of making you happy.

DIALOGUE VIII.

MOTHER. I have a few things yet to tell you, Robert, about the muscles, that will show you still more of the *design, and skill, and goodness of God*, in making them as he has done.

Robert. I shall listen to you, mother, very attentively. Many things that you tell me, are a great deal more entertaining than what I read in my story books.

M. I am glad to hear you say so, my son. Think, too, how much more useful it is for you to learn *what is true*, and what shows you the power, and wisdom, and goodness of our heavenly Father, than to read stories which are not true, and which often have not much in them that is improving or useful. But come, we must begin to talk about the muscles.

Tie your handkerchief again to the handle of the lock on the door.

(Robert does so.)

Now unlatch the door, and pull it open gently, by pulling your handkerchief.

After you stop pulling the handkerchief, does the door shut again?

R. No, mother, and it will not, unless I push it to, again.

M. Suppose, I should tie my handkerchief to the other handle of the lock, on the outside, and I should stand in the entry, and pull my handkerchief after you had done pulling yours.

R. You would pull the door to, mother.

M. Stretch out your arm as far as you can, Robert, so as to have your hand just as high up from the floor, as your shoulder is.

(Robert does do.)

M. Bend your arm at the elbow, so as to have your hand touch your breast.

R. I thought to have it done, mother, and you see, my hand went to my breast immediately.

M. You see, it stops there, and does not go back again. The muscles inside of your arm, about which I have told you, contracted, and pulled your hand to your breast. But this same muscle cannot pull your hand back again, any more than your handkerchief, when you stood *inside of the door*, could pull it so as to make it shut.

R. Then, mother, there must be an *outside muscle*, on the arm, to straighten it again, after I bend it at the elbow.

M. You are right, Robert; there are two such muscles, and they are very strong ones. For if you will try, you will find, that, after having bent your arm, you can straighten it with a great deal of force.

If you lift your whole arm up, at the shoulder joint, and then let it fall down itself, it will do so, just as the lid of a trunk does, if you let go of it, after having raised it up.

But very often, in different kinds of work, men

want to bring the hand down quickly, and so as to strike a hard blow. They want to do so, when they cut wood, and when they drive nails with a hammer.

The outside muscles of the arm enable them to do this; and here again, you see *the design* which God had in making these muscles, and in placing them just right to pull, *exactly*, in an opposite direction from that in which some other muscles pull. *Unless they had pulled just in this manner, they would have been of no use.*

R. Do you remember, mother, when the two men came to saw wood for us, how quick they did it. They had one long saw, with handles at each end, and they stood on different sides of a stick of wood, and, first, one man pulled the saw towards *him*, and then the other man pulled it towards *him*, and so they kept pulling it backwards and forwards. Do not the muscles about which you have been telling me, pull in some such way?

M. They do, my son, and they are called *antagonist muscles*. There are a great many of them in our bodies. All the motions of our hand and fingers are made with their help; and without them, most of the motions that we make, would be very awkward;—many of them quite useless; and some motions that we should very often want to make, we could not make at all.

R. One thing, mother, about the muscles, I do not understand.

M. What is that, my son?

R. I understand pretty well, how they pull the bones whenever they shrink; but, mother, what makes them shrink, just exactly when I think to have any part of my body move?

M. Yes, my son; and what makes them contract, *slowly or quickly*, just as you think to have the motion slow or quick; and, then to *stop contracting*, just when you wish to have the motion stop; and to stop *just as long* as you wish to have them; and then to let the *antagonist muscles* pull the other way, just when you think to have them do so!

Is not this very wonderful, indeed, when you think, how many thousand times your muscles do all this, even in one day?

R. It is, mother. I think, it is the most wonderful thing that you have yet told me. Do explain it to me.

M. I know hardly any thing about it, Robert. The wisest men who have studied about it a great deal, are as ignorant as you and I are, and cannot explain it.

All that they know is, that there are a great many cords, or strings, made up of very fine threads, that go from a part of the head called the *brain*,—and also from the *inside* of the back-bone, which is filled with something that is connected with the brain,—all over the body; and that, without these cords, we could not see, nor hear, nor smell, nor taste, nor feel; —and that without them, the muscles would not contract, when we wish any part of the body to move.

R. What are these cords called, mother?

M. They are called *nerves*. They run into the muscles, and alongside of the smaller bundles and threads of the muscles; so that every muscle has a great many of these nerves.

Now, when you think to have your hand bend at the wrist; *your thinking somehow or other by the help of the brain, and of the nerves which go to the muscle that bends your wrist, makes that muscle contract, and immediately your wrist is bent.*

How the nerves help to do this, or how they make the muscles contract, nobody knows. The wisest men only know, that it is so; but of *the way in which it is done*, they are just as ignorant as a little child.

They have found out, that if the nerves belonging to any muscle are weakened or destroyed by sickness or disease, then *that muscle* will not contract as it did before, although the person thinks, and wishes ever so much, to have that part of the body move, which the muscle was made to move.

The nerves do the errand from the mind to the muscle; and the muscle will not obey the mind, unless the nerves are well and strong, and do the errand faithfully.

R. God knows, mother, how the nerves make the muscles contract.

M. Yes, my son, for he made them both; and he made them to act together as they do.

If I had time to explain to you about *all the nerves in the body;* how some go to your eye, and help you to see; and some to your ear, and to your nose, and to your tongue, and help you to hear, and smell, and taste; and a great many others to all parts of your body, so that you have feeling all over it; and then, how a great many others go to all the muscles, and help you to make all the different kinds of motions that you do; you would wonder still more and more at the wisdom, and skill, and goodness, of God, and see *his design*, in making all these curious parts of your body just as he has made them.

R. Mother, do tell me about some other parts of the body. I suppose, there are some more curious than any you have told me about yet.

M. There are so, Robert; but I believe you must wait till you grow a little older, for, then, you will understand the explanations of the different parts of the body much better than you can now.

But I have one thing more to tell you about the nerves and muscles, to show you how wonderfully God has made them to *work together*, for our benefit.

R. What is that, mother?

M. Do you ever know what I mean, *when I do not speak to you?*

R. Sometimes, I can guess what you mean, mother, *from your looks*. I can easily tell whether you are glad or sorry, and whether you are pleased with me or not. It always makes me feel sorry to see *you look so.*

M. Suppose, I should always wear a veil over my face, so that you could not see it, when I was talking with you.

R. O! I should not like that, at all, mother. I like to see your eyes move about, and the different parts of your face move, and look so differently, at different times.

When you tell me stories, or explain things to me, I can understand you much better when I see your face, and look straight at you, in your eyes.

M. That is true, my son; and I can almost always tell, whether you have got up a pleasant, and good boy, by *your looks*, when I first see you in the morning.

And when you was a little infant, you could not speak and tell me, that you were in pain, or felt uneasy, but I knew if you were, by *looking at your face.*

And you learned a great deal, at that time, by *looking at my face.* You could not understand my words; but you very soon began to understand my looks.

R. O! mother, do you not remember, when we were at aunt Mary's, how my little cousin Jane, would look, and look, right at her face, for a great while.

M. Yes, my son; and you remember, too, that when Jane fretted and cried, when nothing was the matter, how your aunt would *look a little cross at her*, and shake her head, and Jane would be still, almost instantly.

R. Yes, mother, and often I am more afraid of you, *when you only look at me*, than I am, when you speak to me for doing wrong.

M. And when you are a good boy, and I pat you on the cheek, and *look pleasantly* at you, how do you feel then?

R. I feel very happy, mother; *I like to see your looks, then.* It almost seems, as if you were speaking to me, and saying, that you love me for being a good boy.

But I know another time, mother, when *your looks* did me a great deal of good.

M. When was that?

R. When I was so sick on my little bed, and you had to send for the doctor. You sat by me, and took hold of my hand, and *looked as if you felt sorry for me*, and wished to do every thing to make me better. I think *your looks really did me a great deal of good.*

M. And you remember, too, Robert, what a kind man the doctor was.

R. Oh! yes; *he looked very kindly at me*, and that, too, made me feel better, and hope I should get well. Mother, I think, doctors should take a great deal of care, always to look pleasantly and kindly, when they go to see people who are sick.

M. We should all of us, my son, try to look pleasantly and kindly, at all times; and then, we shall, both, make others happier, and feel more happy ourselves.

The doctor, too, is often able to learn a great deal *from the looks of the persons who are sick*, when he sees them, the first time; and to tell, when he sees them afterwards, whether they are getting better or worse.

R. Mother, I never knew, before, how useful it is, to have our faces look so many different ways, and show what we think and what we feel.

M. God knew, my son, how necessary it would be, for our comfort, that it should be so, and you see how curiously, and with what wonderful design and skill, he has made the different parts of the face, and the muscles and nerves, which help these parts to move, in so many different ways.

R. Mother, are there a good many muscles to move our eyes, and all the different parts of our face?

M. There are, my son, and by their help we can look almost, if not quite, as many different ways, as we can think, or feel.

How many different ways a little child moves his mouth and lips, when he feels pleasant or unpleasant; kind or cross; mild or angry; patient or impatient; contented or fretful; when he smiles, or laughs, or pouts, or cries.

How many different ways, too, he moves his mouth and lips, when he breathes, and speaks, and chews, and swallows.

To open and move the mouth and lips, in all the different ways that we can, a number of muscles is necessary. Now, when one of these *pulls one way*, you know, there must be another muscle, to pull back again, *the other way*, which, you recollect, I told you, is called, an *antagonist muscle*.

R. I hardly see, mother, how there can be room for so many different muscles, and the antagonist muscles, too, about the mouth and lips.

M. The truth is, Robert, there is only *one antago-*

nist muscle, which is so curiously made and placed, that it can pull all sorts of ways, so as to pull back all the other muscles, by itself alone.

R. Where is it placed mother?

M. It is all round the mouth, about an inch in breath. It is the thick, fleshy part of the lips. It lies in the red part of the lips, and it is fastened at the two corners of the mouth. Its use is to be an antagonist muscle to a great many others that move the mouth and lips, and to shut up the mouth so tight, if you blow ever so hard, it can keep the breath in your mouth.

R. How far it can be stretched, mother, and then how small it can contract itself!

M. Yes, it is both a very elastic, and a very strong muscle. *It is round*, for a straight muscle could not have pulled so many different ways, and it is placed *just where* a round muscle was wanted. It helps too, to form part of the mouth and lips; and there are a good many letters and words which we could not speak, if we did not have this curious muscle.

R. How many, many different things had to be made, and exactly put together, mother, to make our bodies just what they should be!

M. That is true, my son; I might keep on explaining to you, *even about the muscles alone*, and every one of them, would show you the wonderful design, and contrivance, and skill, and great goodness, too, of the Almighty Being who made us.

But we have talked enough, for this time. I shall tell you a little more about the muscles and nerves, this evening.

DIALOGUE IX.

Robert. Is there any other *round muscle*, mother, besides the one that goes round the mouth?

Mother. Yes, there is one that goes all round the eye. It lies directly under the skin of the upper and lower eyelids, and is very flat and thin. It is fastened to a little knob on the upper jaw bone, quite in the inner corner of the eye, close to the nose. If you put your finger carefully there, you will feel the tendon, which fastens it, like a little knot.

It goes from this tendon over the upper eyelid, round the outer corner of the eye, over the lower eyelid, and so, back again, to the tendon.

This curious little muscle helps us to shut up the eye, which, you know, we often want to do; and if any thing gets into the eye, it squeezes very hard, and often squcezes it out.

When persons weep, it is this muscle, too, which presses the ball of the eye down, and squeezes something like a small piece of spongy flesh, that makes the tears, and they flow out.

R. Mother, it seems to make me feel easier, sometimes, to weep.

M. Yes, my son, there are times when our pain, or our sorrow, causes us to weep, and it is a great relief to us, to shed tears.

God knew that it would be so, and he made this curious muscle, and the small piece of spongy flesh, which is called a *gland*, and the other parts of the eye, so that we might get this relief.

I knew a lady who could not shed a tear, even when she was in the greatest pain or sorrow. The gland, which makes the tears, had been destroyed by severe sickness; and although she often tried to weep, and strained the muscle, about which I have been telling you, as hard as she could, she could not shed a single tear. She told me, she did not know before that severe sickness, how exceedingly distressing it was, never to be able to weep. She said, oh! how much she would give, to be able to weep, sometimes!

A friend of mine was acquainted with a gentleman in England, who could not open his right eye, unless he raised the eyelid with his fingers. This was quite an affliction to him. His right eye was perfectly sound, and when the eyelid was raised, he could see as well with that eye, as with the other.

R. What was the reason of that, mother?

M. The muscle which lifts up the eyelid, or the nerve which helps the muscle to move, was weakened, or destroyed.

So you see, how much your comfort depends upon all these muscles and nerves, even the smallest of them, which God has so curiously made and put together, and which he so kindly keeps in perfect order.

Watches, you know, often get quite out of order; and even the very best of them, will not always go exactly right. We are obliged to send them to a skillful watchmaker, and have them put in order again.

Now, our bodies are made up, of a thousand, and thousand times more parts than a watch has,—and much more curious parts too, more difficult to put together, and to have them all fit each other, and *always go right.*

R. Mother, I think no parts of a watch are any thing like so curious, as the muscles and nerves.

M. That is true, my son; and when we consider, how perfectly all the parts of our body are made, and put together, *for the thousand different uses for which they were designed,*—and, still more, that in most persons, *they keep on going exactly right,* what is the contrivance and skill of the man who makes a watch, to that of the Creator and Preserver of our bodies!

R. I wonder, people do not think more of this, mother!

M. It is, indeed, not only wonderful, my son, but, it shows, how stupid and ungrateful they are.

How thankful most persons would be, if any body should give them a beautiful, gold watch, that cost a hundred dollars, and was one of the best that could be made.

They would be often looking at it, and admiring it, and showing it to others, and talking about it, and feeling very thankful to the kind friend who gave it to them.

Our arm and hand is a vastly more wonderful, and useful instrument to us, than the dearest and best watch would be, and yet, how seldom we think of this, or talk about it, and feel grateful to our kind Heavenly Father, who made this part, and all the parts, of our bodies for our use and comfort!

R. Mother, I think about it a good deal.

M. I hope, you will continue to do so, my son, and to feel more and more thankful to God, for all his goodness to you.

R. Mother, you have been telling me about many of the muscles in the face; I should think there must be a great many nerves, to go with them, and to help them to act.

M. There are so, Robert, and here is a drawing, in which you will see a good many of them.

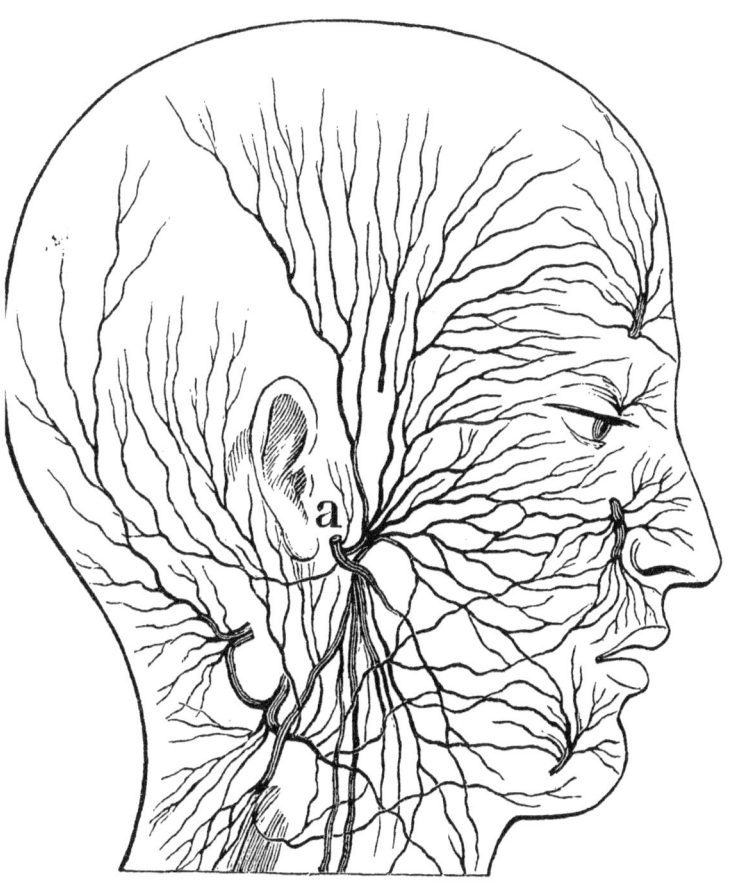

R. Mother, this side of the face is full of them; are there as many on the other side?

M. Just as many, exactly, and they go in different directions, just as these do.

R. Do they all do the same thing?

M. No, my son, some of them go to the eyes, that we may see; and some to the ears, that we may hear; and some to the nose, that we may smell; and some to the tongue, that we may taste; and some to the mouth, and lips, and throat, that we may eat, and swallow, and speak; a good many go to all parts of the face, so that we may feel, if any thing hurts us, and put it away, or, if the face is wounded or injured, take care of it; some of the nerves go to muscles, and help them to move, *even if we do not think to have them move;* and most of these, and some others, also, *tell the muscles to move*, whenever we wish to have them do so.

R. How do muscles move, mother, when we do not think to have them move?

M. Does a little child think to draw in the air and blow it out again, every time that he breathes?

R. No, mother, and *you* do not, nor I. But I can stop breathing, if I choose.

M. Yes, for a very little while. But, if you were to try to do so long, you would find, that you would soon have to breathe again, in spite of yourself.

R. You told me, mother, that a hundred muscles are moved, every time that we breathe.

ON NATURAL THEOLOGY.

M. I did so; and you see, that not only one muscle, but a hundred, are moved continually, without our thinking to have them move?

R. But what is the use, mother, in having *any of the muscles of the face move*, if we do not think to have them move?

M. Did you ever *wink your eyes, without thinking of doing it?*

R. Yes, mother, a great many times. They keep winking constantly. Why do they keep winking so?

M. You remember, I told you about the tears, and about that something like a small piece of spongy flesh, called a gland, which makes the tears.

Tears are very useful for something more, than to give us relief by weeping. They moisten the eye, and keep it clean and smooth, so that it moves easily.

The tears keep coming all the while from the gland, through a great many small tubes, which run in the upper eyelid and they are spread, by *the motion of this eyelid, and the lower one*, when they wink, all over the forepart of the eye.

If more tears come than are needed to moisten and to clean the eye, they are carried through two very little holes in the eyelids, to a small bag, near the inside corner of the eye, and then through a hole in the bone, as large as a goose-quill, to the inside of the nose.

They are, then, spread over the inside of the nostril, and the warm air, that is all the while, passing up and down, as we breathe, dries them up, almost instantly.

But there is another reason, why your eyelids wink of themselves. It is to keep off any thing that may be coming too near to the eye, to hurt it,—any little insect, or any little particles of dust. The eyelashes, too, were made for the same purpose.

So that you see, in how many different ways, God has taken care that the eye should be kept in order, and be kept safe from injury.

But this is not the one hundredth part of what is most curious and wonderful, that I could tell you, about the eye. You shall read all about it when you grow older, and are better able to understand it. For some things about it, it would be very difficult, indeed, if not impossible, for you to understand now.

R. When I grow a few years older, I mean to study all about the different parts of the body, if you will let me.

M. I shall have no objection, my son, especially if you should be a physician; but you must be very industrious, and learn a good many other things, first.

R. Mother, I want to ask you one question about the nerves.

M. Do, my son, as many as you choose.

R. You have showed me a drawing of the nerves which go all over the face. Do *all these nerves* help us to look so very differently, at different times?

M. No, my son, it is only *one set of them* which is principally concerned in doing this. You see the branch of nerves which is just before the ear (a). (See page 107.) That is the one which, somehow or other, makes the muscles move that draw the parts of the face, *when we look so differently, at different times.*

Those different looks are called *expressions,* and when a person has them often, and so as to show strongly what he means, or what he feels, we say *he has an expressive countenance.*

R. Mother, I like to see an expressive countenance, for, then, I can understand people much better.

M. That is true, Robert. *The expressions of the countenance, seem to be the very coming out of the soul.*

Many animals, you know, have no such expressions of face at all; and none of them have any thing like the different kinds,—the beauty, the strength, and the meaning, which the expressions of the human face have.

R. Mother, a dog sometimes has meaning in his face.

M. He has, Robert, but only think how much more, a human face has.

A dog expresses a very few things by his face. A man can express,—oh! how many different kinds of thoughts, and feelings, in his countenance.

If you will examine the faces of different animals, you will see considerable difference in their expressions. Some, you know, have a cross look, and others a pleasant and kind look. Some, too, seem to have much more meaning in their faces than others.

But, after all, none of them can express such a variety of thoughts and feelings, in their faces, as we can in ours.

When you take a walk, look attentively at the faces of different animals, and compare their expressions with the countenances of men, women, and children, and you will see how much truth there is in what I have been telling you.

Here is a picture of a human face, and of a dog's. See how much more of soul there is in the former, than in the latter.

ON NATURAL THEOLOGY. 113

R. I have often been amused, mother, to see the deaf and dumb talking with each other, they have so many different kinds of expressions in their countenances.

M. If they had not, my son, they could not understand each other as well as they do; and they could not understand each other, at all, about some things.

R. I should think, mother, their teachers would, sometimes, grow very tired—*they* have to make so many different kinds of expressions of countenance.

M. I dare say they do; but without all these different expressions, it would be quite impossible to teach the deaf and dumb the meaning of a great many words; so that they would not be able to learn how to read and write.

R. God has been very kind to them, mother, in

making so many muscles and nerves, for the face, to give it expression.

M. He has, my son; *and this,* I think, *is the most wonderful part of the human body, and shows more than any other, the design, the contrivance, the skill, and the goodness, of God.*

When you see the picture of Abraham offering up Isaac, in the parlor, do you think it could have been made by chance?

R. No, mother. Chance, sometimes, makes something like trees and houses, on the panes of glass, in the winter, when they are covered with frost; but I know, that chance could never make any thing, at all, like that picture of Abraham and Isaac.

M. It is not proper, Robert, to say that chance makes, even, the little trees and houses, on the windows, in winter. It is God who makes the cold, and the frost, just so as to have the glass covered with all the different shapes of things, that you see.

If you were to take a handful of little pins, and throw them up, in the air, over the table, and they should fall down upon it, into beautiful shapes of houses, and trees, and animals,—that might be said to happen by chance.

R. It could never happen so, mother.

M. If once in a hundred times, Robert, one shape should look a little like a house, or a tree, or, once in ten thousand times throwing them up, one should look like an elephant, you would wonder at it very much.

R. I should, mother, but I do not wonder at merely seeing a picture, *because I know, a painter made it.*

M. But do you not wonder at the skill of the painter, in giving such fine, and meaning, expressions to the countenances of Abraham and Isaac?

R. I do, mother, it has made me weep, sometimes, to look at it.

M. Now, think, Robert, how long the painter had to be learning; how much he had to notice the human countenance; and how many pictures he had to draw, and how he had to keep slowly improving himself, till at last, he was able to draw the picture which you know every body admires so much.

R. Did it take him a year to do all this, mother?

M. Yes, my son, many years; and, I dare say, if he could see the picture now, he could show you some things in it, that he could make better.

Then, think, that in making this picture, he had first to design it,—how he would draw Abraham and Isaac, and how he would make them look. He had, too, to prepare all his paints, of many different colours, and his brushes, of different sizes, very nicely; and when he began to draw, he had to do it very carefully; and often to stop and think; and he had to put on a little more paint in one place, and in another, or some of a different colour, before he could get it to suit him; and, then, he had to go back from the drawing and look at it, and make some more alterations; and, after working, in this slow and patient way, for a long time, he had to ask some friends to look at it, and to tell him, if it had any faults; and, then he had to go to work again, and try to remove these faults; and so, after months of thought and labour, he made the beautiful picture which you now see.

If this picture shows you, from the design, and contrivance, and skill, which appear in it, *that it must have been made by some one*, and by a painter who had a great deal of design, and contrivance, and skill,—*what must we think, when we see so many hundreds and thousands of human countenances, and even those of little children, having so many different, and fine expressions?*

R. We cannot but think, mother, that some one made them, and gave them these expressions. *We know, that God did it*, and that his design, and skill, and contrivance, in doing it, were very, very great, indeed.

M. Yes, my son, and there is *one thing*, in which the human countenance far, far exceeds that drawn by the most skilful painter.

R. What is that, mother?

M. The painter can give the face that he draws,

but *one, single expression*, and that remains always the same.

R. But the human face has the power of changing its expressions, as quick as we can think, or feel.

Should the painter wish to give a new expression to the face which he has drawn, he must work at it again; or, what is more probable, he must draw a new one.

The motion of a few nerves and muscles, in an instant, gives new expressions to our faces, and speaks, before we can think of it, the language of our souls.

DIALOGUE X.

Mother. I have something more to say to you, my son, of the curious and wonderful way in which God has made our faces, so that they can speak the language of our souls.

Robert. Mother, have the beasts such muscles and nerves as we have, to give expression to their faces?

M. That was one thing which I am going to tell you. Some of them have some muscles and nerves, in their faces, like ours; but none of them as many; and most of them have very few, indeed.

R. That is the reason, I suppose, mother, why they have so little meaning in their faces.

M. It is one reason. Besides, you know, they have no soul like ours. They do not think and feel, as we do. They have no feelings about what is right and wrong. But, even, if they had a soul like ours, it could not show itself, its thoughts and its feelings, on their faces, as our souls do; because they have not the muscles and nerves, that are necessary to give all kinds of expression to the face.

R. I am very glad, mother, that God has made our faces so different from those of the beasts.

M. Yes, my son, and if it were not so, only think how stupid and dull we should all look.

The little infant would not, as it does now, delight to look and look at its mother's face; and *there first begin to learn*, that its mother loves it dearly,—is glad, when it is happy,—and is sorry, when it is in pain.

And the little infant would not learn the meaning of a great many words which are spoken to it; if the looks of the person who speaks to it, did not help it to understand the meaning of the words.

If the little infant, too, did not smile, and weep, and look happy, and look troubled; how difficult it would often be for the mother to know when it was well, or sick; easy or in pain.

How could parents govern their children; if they did not show by their eye, and by their looks, when they are pleased, and when they are displeased,— and when *they really mean*, that the children shall do just as they are told to do.

R. Mother, you know, I went to school, a little while, when you took a short journey.

M. I remember it; but what then?

R. The master said hardly any thing, at all, to make the scholars mind him. But he kept looking about, all the while; and his eye, and his looks, and a little shake of his head, and, sometimes, of his finger, kept the whole school in order.

M. It would be well, my son, if all who keep school, would learn to do as he did.

Here, you see, is another very important purpose, for which God made the human face to have so many different kinds of expression,—*that one person might be the better able to govern others.*

And if our faces did not have these different kinds of expression how difficult it would, often, be for us to know whether others felt happy, to see us happy, or sorry, to see us sorry.

To feel so, is called sympathy, and when persons feel so, we say, that *they sympathize with us.* How miserable we should be, if no one ever sympathized with us, when we are in trouble! And, if we are ever so happy, who wishes to be happy all alone?

Suppose, when your aunt comes to see you, after not having seen you for a long time, and shakes hands with you, and kisses you,—her face should have no more expression than that of your sister's little doll.

R. I should not think the kiss was worth much, mother.

M. Or, suppose, when the doctor came to see you, he had looked, as if he did not feel at all sorry, that you were sick,—but only came to tell what must be done for you, just as you, sometimes, tell Tray to go and drive the ducks away from the kitchen door.

R. I am afraid, mother, it would have made me more sick.

M. Well, so I could go on, Robert, to tell you of a great many other ways in which it is very important, and useful, and pleasant, that our faces should have many different kinds of expression; so, that if they did not, we should feel very uncomfortable, and often miserable, in seeing, and talking with, our fellow men.

And, if different faces had not different looks, do you think, we could always tell one person from another?

R. We might, some persons, mother, because their

faces are larger, or smaller, or lighter, or darker, or are shaped differently.

M. That is true; but I think, there are but few that we should always know in these ways.

Almost every body has some looks, and expressions which belong to himself, which *he* commonly has, and which others do not have, or not so commonly as he has.

It is this which principally helps us to know the same person at all times, and to know different persons, so as not to mistake one for another.

Did you ever think, how many mistakes we should be constantly making, and how much trouble and confusion there would be, if we could not, very soon, tell one person from another?

R. I never did, mother, but I see it now. People, then, would look to us, just as a flock of sheep do,—a great many of them, exactly alike.

M. Yes, my son; and thus, you see, that there is still another important reason, why God has given so many different looks, and expressions, to human faces, —and in doing it, he shows you his wonderful design, contrivance, skill, and goodness.

R. It is, indeed, wonderful, mother, that while there are thousands and millions of people in the world, hardly any two of them look exactly alike. It is strange, that I never thought of this before.

M. It is so common a thing, that we do not think of it. But it is not the less wonderful, because it is common. Often the most common things show us most of the wisdom and goodness of God, and this is one of them.

How wonderful! Here is a *soul*, or *spirit*, within us, not like any thing that we can see, or hear, or smell, or taste, or touch,—but *wholly unlike it*. This soul is in a body, made up of a thousand, curious, different parts. These parts are made, and put together, so as to be exactly suited to each other, and to the whole body. Nothing is in the wrong place; and nothing goes wrong; unless the body is sick, or is hurt.

All this is done, that the body may eat, and drink, and sleep, and live;—just as the bodies of beasts do? Oh! no. This curious body is made, and kept alive, and all its parts in order, that it may be a proper and convenient body for the soul to be in, and use for its own improvement, and comfort, and happiness, and for *that of others*.

For our very bodies are so made, as to show us that God designed, that we should live and act not for ourselves alone, but for others,—and, that we should do all we can, to make each other good, and happy.

The muscles and nerves of the face, are one very striking proof of this.

You have seen what some of them were made for,

to give expression to the face, and *for this purpose only.*

How wonderful! the soul, that *immaterial something* within us, showing its secret thoughts and feelings, on a part of our *material* body,—by the help of a great many, curious nerves and muscles, that move the face in a thousand different ways;—sometimes when we think to have them move so, and sometimes when we do not.

This soul thus shows its thoughts and feelings, that they may be seen, and understood, and felt, by other souls, like itself, dwelling in other bodies, like the body in which it dwells.

And, thus, these souls are the better able to know each other; to converse with each other; to sympathize with each other; to aid each other; and to make each other good and happy.

Who but the *Infinite and Eternal mind,—the Great Spirit, whom we call God,*—could have so made our souls and bodies, and given these wonderful powers of expression to our faces?

Who that looks on the human face, can doubt, for one moment, that there is a God of great power, and wisdom, and skill, and goodness?

R. I am sure, *I* cannot, mother, and I do not think, that any body else can.

M. You see, my son, not only the design, and

contrivance, and skill of God, in having made your face as he has; but *his goodness*, also, in making its various expressions, the means of your own happiness, and of that of others.

Remember how ungrateful you are for all this goodness, and what a bad use you make of your curious and wonderful countenance, when you think and feel wrong; and these wrong thoughts and feelings show themselves in your countenance—and thus make yourself even more unhappy, and others unhappy, too, in looking at you.

R. Mother, you know the man that struck me, in the street, one day, what an ugly-looking face he has.

M. Yes, and do you learn from it, not to have any wrong thoughts and feelings. He has been so often angry, and in a great rage, that now, he looks angry almost all the time. He can hardly look pleasant, if he tries.

ON NATURAL THEOLOGY.

R. How different uncle John looks, mother.

M. And why, Robert? Because he has, for a long time, had kind and benevolent feelings—desiring to love and obey God, and to do good to others. Peaceful and happy himself, and delighted to make and to see others so.

Do you endeavor to feel, and to do so. Pray to God to enable you to feel, and to do so. Never *even think of saying any thing that is not true.* Be frank, and tell what you know, whenever you ought to tell it; and if at any time, persons ask you to tell them things which you ought not to tell them, refuse to do it, mildly, but firmly. Strive against all wrong thoughts and feelings. Endeavor to have kind and generous ones. Seek to make others happy. Above all, love, fear, and obey God; and *look-*

ing to him for help, endeavor to do your duty. Then, be afraid of nothing, and of nobody.

When you are speaking to others, look them full in the face. Do not try to hide your feelings. Let them show themselves in your countenance. Let your eye, and your countenance, have all the expression which your feelings would give.

Do all this. Try to do it. And your face will acquire *habits of expression* that will make you feel happy yourself, and increase the happiness of others.

In this way, you will best show your thankfulness to God, for giving you the *power of expression*, in your countenance, and you will make that *use of this power*, which will do the most good to yourself, and to others.

R. Mother, will you be so good as to tell me, when I have any cross or unpleasant looks, so that I may try to look differently.

M. I am glad to hear you ask me to do that, my son. But have right thoughts and feelings, and there will be but little danger of your face ever having unpleasant expressions.

But dinner is ready, and we must stop talking.

DIALOGUE XI.

Robert. Mother, I have been to see an elephant, this morning. Uncle John took me.

Mother. It was very kind in him to do so. And what do you think of the elephant, Robert? Does this picture look like his head?

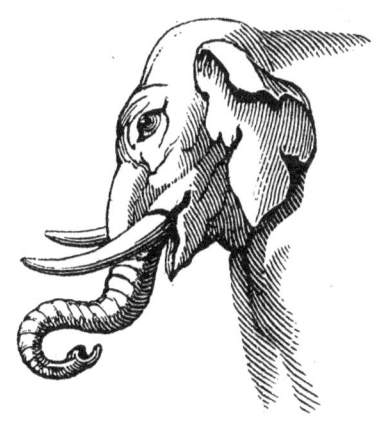

R. Yes, exactly. He is a very wonderful animal, mother. I thought, at first, he looked very ugly and frightful, he was so large and heavy, and clumsy. I was a good deal afraid of him. But, pretty soon, when the keeper spoke to him, and told him to do some things, I found that he was very gentle, and kind, and that he was not so awkward as I, at first, thought he was. He could not do much, though, if he had not that long trunk.

M. *That long trunk*, Robert, is one more, very striking proof of the design, and contrivance, and skill of our Heavenly Father.

He has taken care, in a great variety of ways, to provide for the wants, and for the comfort of beasts, and birds, and fishes, and insects, as well as for ours. And as *the end* for which he made them, is very different from that for which he made us, so he has given them bodies different from ours; and bodies exactly suited to the different places and ways, in which they live.

R. Yes, mother, how different a bird is made from a fish.

M. True, my son, and how many different kinds of birds there are; and in many things, how different they are made from each other, so as to be suited to their different ways of living, and to the country, and to the climate in which they live.

Just so it is with beasts, also. There are a great many different kinds, and each kind has *something peculiar to itself*, to lead us to admire the wisdom, and power, and goodness of God.

R. The elephant, mother, has something very peculiar, indeed,—that long trunk of his!

M. Yes, and the elephant has great need of his trunk. He would be very helpless without it.

The neck of four-footed animals is usually long, in proportion to the length of their legs, so that they may be able to stoop down, and reach their food, on the ground, without difficulty.

R. Mother, I should think, some animals would get very tired, holding their heads down, as long as they do, to get their food.

M. It would be so, my son; but God has provided something to prevent this difficulty.

There is a tough, strong, tendon-like strap, braced from their head to the middle of the back, which supports the weight of the head; so that, although it is large and heavy, it may be held down long, without any pain, or uneasiness.

We do not have this strap, because we do not need to bend our head in the same way as beasts do. Our heads are sufficiently supported without it.

God provides such things, only when they are necessary; and this shows, how he has design in every thing that he makes.

The elephant, as you saw, is a very tall animal, and his head is a good way from the ground; and yet his neck is very short, so that he cannot, without kneeling, or lying down, bring his mouth to the ground.

This short neck, so different from that of other animals, whose heads are far from the ground, has one great advantage. It makes it so much the easier for the elephant to support the weight of his very large head and heavy tusks.

But somehow or other, the difficulty of having so short a neck, especially in getting food and drink, was to be remedied. And the admirable trunk, which God designed, and made, on purpose for the elephant, removes entirely all this difficulty. Still more, it has many advantages, and very great ones too, over the long necks of other animals.

R. I saw the elephant do some things with his trunk, mother, which other animals could not do, with their long necks, and teeth, and paws, all together.

But do tell me a little more particularly about the trunk. Is it bone, or flesh, mother?

M. It is not bone, my son; it is a hollow, fleshly tube, made of muscles and nerves, and covered with a skin of a blackish color, like that of the rest of the body.

R. There must be a great many muscles in it, I should think, mother, or the elephant could not make so many different kinds of motions with it.

M. You are right, Robert. Mr. Cuvier, a very learned man, in France, who knew a great deal, and who wrote several curious books, about the different kinds of animals, tells us, that he has found, *there are more than thirty thousand distinct muscles in the trunk of an elephant!*

R. Oh! mother, if he was not a good man, I should almost think, he says what is not true.

M. There is no reason, my son, to doubt the truth of what he tells us. There are some things, even more wonderful than this, in some little insects.

There is a small kind of caterpillar, that has four thousand muscles, in its little body.

But there is something about the eyes of some insects, yet more wonderful.

A common fly, such as we see about the house, does not move its eyes, as we do. They are fixed fast in its head, and do not turn. But this difficulty is remedied by a very curious contrivance. Each eye is made up of a great many little eyes; something like what you have seen in the stopple of a decanter, so that when you look through it, you seem to see a great many of the same kind of thing.

These little eyes are hemispheres, or half balls, and they are so placed, that they look different ways; so that the fly can look about, sometimes through one, and sometimes through another, and see nearly, if not quite, as well as we can with our eyes.

In the two eyes of a common fly, there are eight

thousand such smaller eyes. In the two eyes of the dragonfly, there are twenty-five thousand such smaller eyes.

Each of these smaller eyes, in the large eye of the fly, and of the dragonfly, *sees perfectly of itself*, in one direction, and is made up of still smaller parts, and has nerves to give it the power of sight.

What must be the fineness of these smaller parts and nerves!

Here is a picture of a very small part of the large eye of a dragon-fly, greatly magnified.

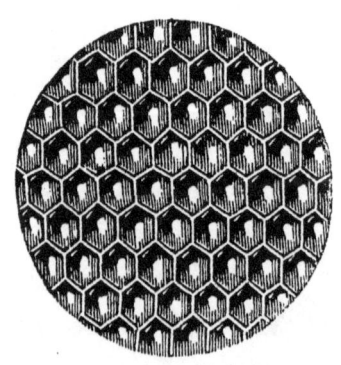

R. How was all this found out, mother?

M. By the help of very powerful microscopes, which magnify things, and make them look, millions of times larger than they really are.

With one kind of microscope that I have seen, a

little insect was magnified five hundred and seventy millions of times.

R. Well, I do not doubt any longer, mother, that there are thirty thousand muscles in the trunk of an elephant.

And how many nerves there must be, to help all these muscles to move, whenever the elephant wishes to have them move.

M. Yes, my son, and it has been found out that the trunk alone has as many nerves as all the rest of the body has.

It is the number, the fineness, and the variety of these nerves, that enable the trunk to do all the curious things that it was made to do.

An elephant that is fourteen feet high, has a trunk about eight feet long, and five feet and a half round, at its thickest part, next the head.

This trunk, as you saw, can be made shorter or longer, as the animal chooses, and can be moved, with great ease, in every possible direction.

It has such prodigious strength, that the elephant can quickly knock a man down with it; and can pull up a tree of moderate size by the roots; and break off the largest branches; and raise very heavy weights.

On the underside, there are some things like little claws, or like the feet of a caterpillar, which take hold of what the elephant wishes to grasp, and help to hold it faster; and at the end of the trunk, the skin is lengthened about five inches, in the form of a finger. With this finger he can pick up a pin from the ground, or the smallest piece of money; he can select herbs and flowers, and take them one by one; he can untie knots; he can open and shut gates, by turning the keys, or pushing back the bolts; and, with this finger, an elephant has been taught to make regular marks, like letters, with an instrument as small as a pen.

In the middle of the finger, there is a hollow place like a cup, and in the bottom of the cup, are two holes, or nostrils, through which the animal smells and breathes.

By placing the edge of the end of his trunk on the surface of any heavy thing, and then suddenly drawing in his breath, so as to get all the air out of the inside of the trunk, the thing he wishes to raise will stick fast to the end of the trunk, and he can lift it up easily.

R. Mother, I wonder if this is not something like what the boys call a sucker?

M. What is that, Robert?

R. Did you never see one, mother? They take a round piece of pretty soft leather, and fasten a stout piece of twine to the middle of it. Then the leather is soaked in water, and put on the top of a large, heavy stone, and pressed down on it very hard with the foot. The boy pulls up the string; the leather rises up a little in the middle, but all round the edges it sticks very tight to the stone; and the stone is lifted up, ever so high, without falling off from the leather.

But if the edge of the leather is pulled up, ever so little, it will come off from the stone, and the string will not raise the stone.

Mother, what is the reason of this? I do not understand it at all.

M. I do not know that I can explain it exactly to you, but I will try.

The air that we breathe, and which is all round us, has weight. It is, all the while, pressing, with equal weight, in all directions. When you are standing, the air presses against the forepart of your body, and against the sides, and against your back, with equal weight.

On every square inch, it presses with a weight equal to fifteen pounds.

On the whole body of a man, it presses with a weight equal to twenty, or thirty, thousand pounds.

If the air pressed upon you, only on the top of your head, it would crush you down to the ground, instantly. If it pressed, only on the forepart of your body, it would throw you down backwards, with great force.

It is because the air presses upon you equally, in all directions, and that it is *inside* of your body, too, that you can stand up, and walk about without difficulty.

If you put a quill, with the end cut square off, to the end of your tongue, and draw the air out of the quill, quickly, it will stick very tight to your tongue.

The reason of this is, that there is no air, *inside of the quill*, to press against the air, *on the outside;* and so the air, all pressing, with great weight, *one way*, on your tongue, and on the outside of the quill, presses them together, and makes the quill stick to the tongue, until the air is, in some way, brought into the inside of the quill again.

In the same way, the leather, about which you told me, is pressed down so hard against the stone, and lies so close to it, that the air, between the leather and the stone, is forced away, so that there is no air there. The leather, when you draw it up with the string, rises a little in the middle, and leaves a hollow place there, in which there is no air. The air, then, on the outside of the leather, and all round, and underneath the stone, presses with great weight, and presses the leather and stone very tight together, because there is no air between them, to press against the air on the outside.

When you lift up the edge of the leather, as you told me, and let the air in, it rushes, with great weight, between the leather and the stone, and they separate from each other.

R. I think, mother, I understand pretty well now, how the elephant, by putting the edge of his trunk on a heavy thing, and then drawing all the air out of it, is able to lift it up, without any difficulty. The air which is under, and all round, the heavy thing, and the trunk, presses them tight together, and makes the heavy thing stick to the trunk.

M. You are right, my son, and when the elephant fills his trunk with air again, this air presses, from the inside of the trunk, against the heavy thing, just as hard, as the air on the outside does, so that there is no force to keep it up, any longer, and it instantly falls down.

With this trunk, the animal takes all his food from the ground, and puts it into his mouth, just as we do ours, with our hand.

When he drinks, too, he first draws up the water into his trunk, and then empties it into his mouth.

R. How many things, mother, he can do with his trunk!

M. Yes, my son, on some accounts, it is even more curious and wonderful than your arm and hand, which I have explained to you.

The trunk of an elephant is to him, what their *neck* is, to other animals.

It is a *nose*, with which he smells and breathes.

It is an *arm* and *hand*, with a very curious *finger*, with which he feels, and does a great many things, easily and quickly.

It has been said that *he carries his nose in his hand;* and it might have been said, also, that he breathes with his hand. How strange it would seem to you and me, if we should smell, and breathe, and feel, and take things, with one of our fingers.

R. Mother, if I go to see the elephant again, I will ask the keeper to let me examine the finger at the end of the trunk, very particularly.

M. I dare say, he will be willing to let you do it.

But I cannot tell you any thing more about the elephant, now.

His trunk, as you have seen, is a most curious instrument, made, in part, to help the animal to get his food; because his neck is so short; and, besides this, to enable him to smell and breathe, and do a great many things which are necessary for his comfort. Do you not think, this is another very striking proof of the design, contrivance, skill, and goodness of God?

R. I do, indeed, mother.

M. Well, my son, men, beasts, birds, fishes, insects, trees, flowers and vegetables, have hundreds, and thousands, of other things quite as wonderful, as any thing that I have yet explained to you. We cannot look around us, without seeing proofs every where, that there is a God, and that he is a Being of infinite power, wisdom, and goodness.

We may well say, as David did, in the Psalms which he wrote:

"O Lord, how manifold are thy works! in wisdom, hast thou made them all: the earth is full of thy riches."

"The Lord is good to all; and his tender mercies are over all his works."

DIALOGUE XII.

MOTHER. I explained to you, yesterday, my son, about the trunk of an elephant, with which he can do a great many things; and how necessary it is for him, that he may get his food and drink.

It is wonderful, to see the many different ways in which beasts, birds, fishes, and insects get their food; and also how God has formed them, that they may do this; and particularly *how their mouths are made*, to take their food after they have found it.

Our mouths are flat. They are made, not to pick up, or take hold of, our food. Our hands do this and put the food into the mouth.

But where animals have no hands, or no trunk, *their mouths* have to pick up, and take hold, of their food. And as their food is of *a great many different kinds*, and found in *a great many different places*, and to be taken, *a great many different ways ;* their mouths had to be made of *a great many different shapes and sizes*, and so as to have *a great many different motions.*

Only think how much design, contrivance, and skill, was necessary to do all this, so as to provide for the comfort, and nourishment, and life, of so many millions of living beings.

Each of them has a mouth, and yet, in how many different ways their mouths are made ; and the mouth of one kind, would be exceedingly inconvenient, and, often, entirely useless, if it had been made for a different kind.

You have seen different kinds of locks ; some for front-doors ; some for parlor-doors ; some for cellar-doors ; some for bureaus ; some for trunks.

R. Yes, mother ; and some, very curious, little padlocks. You know, uncle John has one for his traveling-bag.

M. Well, Robert, these different kinds of locks are

all *alike in some things*, and they were all made, *with one design*, to fasten something up tight; so that it could not be opened without the key.

But when you see them *unlike in other things*, you know, at once, that they were made, *with another design, also*,—to have them suited to things of different sizes and uses, so as to fasten them tight.

R. Yes, mother, and I am sure that a door-lock never was made to be put on to a trunk.

M. When we see, then, so many different kinds of mouths, each suited to a particular kind of animal, that has to get its food in its own way, we are sure that God had a *particular design* in making them so; and this is one, other, striking proof of his wisdom and goodness.

R. Mother, do tell me about some of the curious kinds of mouths that animals have.

M. Did you ever see a wood-pecker?

R. Oh! yes, and I have wondered what he keeps knocking against the tree for, so long, and so hard, with his bill. I should think, he would get very tired sometimes.

M. He is hungry, and is working for his food. You would be glad to work, too, Robert, for your food, if you could not get it, in any other way. And you should be willing to work for it, which, perhaps, you may yet have to do.

R. What is the woodpecker's food, mother?

M. It is, principally, worms and insects, which he finds in the trunks of old, decayed trees.

R. But why does he make so much noise in finding them?

M. The worms and insects are deep in the wood, where other kinds of birds never could reach them.

Here is a drawing of the bill and tongue of the woodpecker, which are made on purpose to enable him to get his food.

His bill is long, straight, hard, and sharp; and like a wedge, at the tip of it. His tongue is round, something like a worm; very long, so that it can come out three or four inches beyond the bill; and has at the end of it a stiff, sharp, bony thorn. This bony end of the tongue has little teeth, as it were, on each side of it, standing backward, like the barb of a fish-hook.

With his bill, he *chisels out* a hole in the wood; and this is what he was doing when you saw him knocking, as you said, and heard the great noise that he made. He keeps chiselling, till he comes to where the worms or insects are; and, then, he suddenly darts out his long tongue upon them; seizes them with the sharp, hooked end of it; and draws them into his mouth.

The wood-pecker chisels a hole, for its nest, in which to lay its eggs; and these holes, often, are very deep, so that the eggs may be safe. The eggs are usually laid on the rotten wood; but, sometimes, moss or wool, is put into the nest, for the eggs to lie on.

You see what contrivance and skill are shown in the bill and tongue of this curious bird. You know the *design* with which they were made,—to enable the wood-pecker to get food, and to make a nest; and you are just as sure that God made them, and made them for this purpose, as that a chisel was made by some one, and that it was made to cut with, into wood. A man has a mallet, to drive a chisel with; but the wood-pecker's head is *his mallet*, and his skull is unusually thick, that his head may bear the jarring which his hard knocks make.

I read, lately, in one of the newspapers, an account

of a wood pecker, somewhere in Massachusetts, which I think will interest you.

He made a deep hole, just as exactly and neatly as if it had been made with a mallet and chisel, to the very centre of the branch of a young, tough, white-oak tree. The branch was from three to five inches round. He did this to find a worm, called a *borer*. The worm had made a hole in the branch, about as large round as a goose-quill, four or five inches below the hole chiseled out by the wood-pecker. The worm was going upward, inside of the branch, when the woodpecker made his hole, just in the right place to catch the worm with his barbed tongue, and devour him.

These worms injure the trees; and the wood-pecker, and other birds, which devour worms and insects, do a great deal of good. It is quite a pity, that they should be killed.

R. Have any other birds, mother, as curious bills, as that of the wood-pecker?

M. Yes, my son; there is a bird called the crossbill, that has this name on account of its bill, the two parts of which are so bent that they cross one another near the point, sometimes on one side, and sometimes on the other, as you see in the picture. The bill is sharp, and single-edged, near the point. They live in cold and mountainous countries, in the forests of fir and pine-trees.

ON NATURAL THEOLOGY. 145

The seeds of the trees are in something of the shape of a cone, or loaf of white sugar, only a good deal smaller, and these cones are full of something like scales. The crossbill divides these scales very dexterously with its bill, and picks out the seed; which it can do, if they are ever so small, by bringing the two pointed ends of its bill exactly together. (Here is a picture of the crossbill.)

Sometimes they have been seen in orchards of fruit-trees, and they will easily divide an apple, so as to get the seeds.

R. Mother, do the bills of birds grow dull by using them?

M. No, my son, unless they live to be very old. I have read of a goldfinch which was twenty-three years old. The people who kept it were obliged, once a week, to scrape its nails and bill, that it might eat, drink, and sit on its bar. It could not fly, and all its feathers had become white.

R. Mother, ducks and geese have very different kinds of bills from those that you have been explaining to me.

M. Yes, they have long, broad bills, somewhat like a spoon, which enables them to get their food under water, and in the ground, and in muddy places. The inside of the bill, near the edges, has rows of short and strong pointed prickles, as you see in the drawing. But they are not teeth to chew with. They are made, to help the bird to find its food. For when the duck plunges its bill down into the water, or mud, it draws them up, and whatever may be in them, through the rows of prickles on the inside of the bill, catching what is good and pleasant for food, and throwing away all the rest.

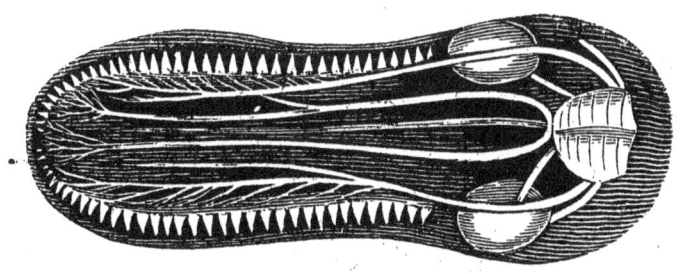

And, that the duck may thus select its food the better, the bill is covered with a skin, and there are large nerves, to give it feeling, which run down quite to the end of it.

How necessary such a kind of bill is for a bird that seeks its food as the duck does, and gropes for it, *out of sight*. As it does not always see its food, it can find it, and tell when it is good and pleasant, by *feeling*.

Here again, how striking is the design, contrivance, and skill, which are shown us, in the bill of the duck, that is made so differently from that of the woodpecker, and of the crossbill, because it has to get its food in a way so different from that in which they get theirs.

There is another bird, called the oyster-catcher, that gets its food in a still different way, and has a bill made so as to be exactly suited to its wants.

Here is a drawing of one.

It lives principally on oysters, and other kinds of shell-fish; the shells of which it opens. That it may be able to do this, it has a long, stout bill, shaped like a wedge; and narrow next to the head, that it may work the more easily in the sand.

These birds not only open the shell-fish with their bill; but if they find one fastened tight to a rock, they will knock it off, as skilfully with their bill, as a man would do with a stone.

R. Mother, is there any thing, like this, as curious about fishes, as there is about birds?

M. Yes, my son, quite so. Indeed, I have read of one fish, that has a way of getting its food, more strange than any thing which I have told you about the birds.

What should you think of a fish shooting flies, as a man does birds, that it may get them to eat?

R. Is that true, mother?

M. Yes, my son. There is a fish that lives in the Indian seas, called a chœtodon, which has a snout like a tube.

R. What is it like, mother, that I have seen?

M. If you cut a quill off square, at both ends, and take the pith out, it will be a small tube. You know you can blow water through it, some distance, and with some force.

The fish has a snout, something like this, through which it can shoot a drop of water, with so sure an aim and with so much force, that it can hit an insect, from four to six feet off, and thus kill it, or stun it, so that it falls down on the water, and the fish gets it for food.

It shoots the insect, too, while it is flying; seldom missing its aim; and this is what very few, even of the most skilful gunners, can do.

These fish have a very beautiful shape, and a great variety of brilliant colors. They are sometimes caught, and kept in a large vessel of water, and amuse the people very much, by their great dexterity, in shooting. For if a fly is put on the edge of the vessel, the fish immediately perceives it, and shoots at it so exactly, as very seldom, indeed, to miss it.

Is all this chance? Strange, indeed, that this fish was made so, and to be able to do so, by chance!

Does a gun chance to be made; and a man chance to find it, and to know what it was made for; and, when he feels hungry, because he has no other food, chance to go into the woods, and chance to keep looking after a bird, to shoot it; and when he sees one, chance to shoot it, and carry it home to eat?

Was there no design, contrivance, and skill, in the making of the gun; and none in the man's using it? Who made the tube-like snout of the chœtodon. and who taught this fish *how to use it?*

R. Mother, he must be a fool, who says, there is no God.

M. Yes, my son, *The fool hath said, in his heart, there is no God.*

It is because they are so wicked, that some men wish to believe, there is no God; and perhaps, in a few instances, have thought that they did believe so.

But they quite forget one thing. If it has happened, by chance, that there are men, with wonderful souls and bodies; and that they have so much design, and skill, and contrivance, as to make the thousands of curious and useful things which we daily see; *it may have happened, that there is a God.*

And if it has happened that there is a God; why may he not have vastly more design, and skill, and contrivance than men have?

How much more a man has, than a dog. It has happened so, at any rate, for we see it, and know it. It has happened, too, that some men have a great deal more wisdom and power than others.

It has happened, that men make curious and wonderful things. May it not have happened, that God made the millions of curious and wonderful things that we see, which we know, men have not made, and which, we also know, *it is impossible for them to make?*

And if so, how vast the wisdom and power of God must be! They are so vast, that we cannot think how vast they are.

It may have happened, then, that *there is a God of infinite wisdom and power.*

The atheist is often afraid, to do certain, wrong things; because he knows, *it may happen*, that his fellow-men will despise him, and avoid him, and have nothing to do with him, or, if the things are bad enough, that they will even put him in prison, or hang him.

All this has often happened to bad men, notwithstanding they were able to hide the wrong things that they did, from the knowledge of every body, for a long time. They may have done this for years, but it has often, very often, happened, that it was found out, at last. They did not expect that it would be so. They felt quite safe. But, at length, they were found out, to their great surprise and shame, and were sadly disgraced and punished.

May it not happen, that *for his sins, even the most secret ones*, the atheist will be punished in a future world? Cannot God find his sins out, if his fellow-men can find them out?

It happens, as the atheist says, by chance, that he often suffers very severe punishment in this world, for doing wrong; may it not happen, that he will suffer, *still more severely*, in the future world? Does chance do so many, wonderful, and right, and good things in this world, and none in the next?

The atheist says, all things have happened, and continue to happen, by chance.

What if it is so? suppose it is so; still he is a very unwise and daring man.

For why is it, as you have seen, any more improbable, that it should happen, that there is an infinitely wise and powerful God, who will punish sin in the future world, than that there are men who have but little wisdom and power, but who yet have prudence and strength enough, to punish each other, when they do wrong in this world?

What a risk, then, the atheist runs! The Bible tells us, that *it is a fearful thing to fall into the hands of the living God.*

How foolish, as well as wicked, are those who doubt that there is a God; or who deny his right to govern them; or who do not love him, and do all he has commanded us to do!

Think of these truths, my son, and may God enable you to understand them, to believe them, and to feel them.

DIALOGUE XIII.

MOTHER. I have told you, Robert, about a fish that shoots water at insects, that are flying above it, and thus gets them for food. Now, I am going to tell you about a fish that has a very curious way of defending itself against the attacks of larger fishes, which come to devour it,—and of preventing resistance in smaller ones, that it wishes to seize for food.

Robert. I suppose it has a very large mouth, and sharp teeth, mother.

M. No, my son, if you were to look at it, you would not see any thing about it that looked, as if the fish had much power to do any thing, only to swim.

It looks like an eel; indeed it is called the *electrical eel*. Look at this drawing of it.

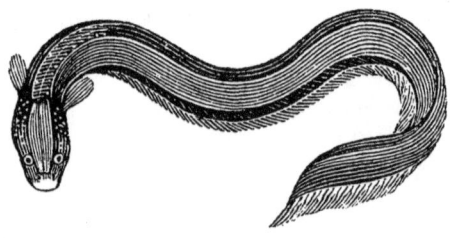

It is very common in South America. It is from three to five feet long, and about a foot round in the thickest part. Some have been found more than twenty feet long, which have such great power, that if a man only touches them, they can kill him instantly.

R. Mother, if I did not know that you never tell me any thing that is not true, I could not believe it.

M. You see, my son, the advantage of always speaking the truth. If I had, sometimes, deceived you, you would not know whether to believe me now or not.

R. Mother, do explain to me about this wonderful fish.

M. I will try to, so far as I can; but there are some things about it which I do not understand myself, and many things, too, which *you cannot understand* till you grow older, and have studied a good many books. But I will explain to you enough to show you, in this curious fish, one more striking proof of the design, contrivance, and skill, of God.

You have seen the lightning.

R. Oh! yes, mother, do you not remember the terrible thunder-storm last summer, when you and I were sitting in the parlour, and, all at once, we saw the lightning strike a tall tree in the field? What a loud clap of thunder there was, at the same time.

M. I remember it very well, my son, and how we went the next day to look at the tree, and saw it split quite through, in the middle, and a good deal burned.

But do you remember, Robert, how strangely we both felt, as if something had struck us, and given us a jar all over?

R. Yes, mother; and you told me, you thought the lightning must have struck the lightning-rod on our house, too, and run down into the ground, without doing the house any harm.

M. In a thunder-storm, my son, the clouds are filled with *something which is called electricity*. It is not known, what it is;—*what it does*, is all that is known.

One cloud, sometimes, has more electricity in it, than another cloud has. If these two clouds come near each other, the electricity will go from the cloud which has the most, to that which has the least. This it does very suddenly; and in passing thus, from one cloud to the other, that bright something, like fire, is seen which we call *lightning;* and soon the noise is heard, which we call *thunder.*

The tree that we saw struck, had less electricity in it, than the cloud which passed over it had. The electricity went suddenly from the cloud to the tree. It appeared in the bright flash of lightning that we saw, and we say, the lightning struck the tree.

About eighty years ago, Dr. Franklin, a countryman of ours, made a kite out of silk, and raised it high up in the air, during a thunder storm.

After some time, the electricity passed from the clouds to the kite, and came down the string, at the end of which was a key. Dr. Franklin put his knuckles to the key, and suddenly bright sparks came from it, to his knuckles.

R. Mother, that was lightning; did it not kill him?

M. No, my son, the quantity was too small, to do him any harm. But, sometimes, there is so much

ON NATURAL THEOLOGY. 157

electricity in a flash of lightning, that when it strikes persons, it kills them instantly.

There is a machine, called an *electrical machine*, a part of which is a large, round, hollow cylinder of glass, that is made to turn round with a handle.

When this is turned round, somehow or other electricity is made, and comes from the glass to a long tube of brass, with a brass ball on the end of it.

If any one puts his knuckle to this brass ball, bright sparks of fire will come from it, just as they did from the key on the string of Dr. Franklin's kite.

R. And does this machine make lightning, mother?

M. Yes, my son, it may be said to do so; for it makes the *same electricity appear*, in *bright sparks*, which the clouds make to appear, in *lightning*, during a thunder storm.

R. Does it not hurt a person, mother, to have the sparks from the brass ball, strike his knuckle?

M. No, my son, very little, if any. But there is a way of getting a great deal of electricity, so as to hurt a person very much, or even to kill him.

A curious vial is made, with a brass rod going into it, and a brass ball at the end of the rod. While the glass cylinder is turned, and the electricity is passing from it, to the long brass tube; if the ball of the vial is held near to the ball of the tube, sparks of electricity will go from the ball of the tube to the ball of the vial. These sparks will keep going, and the electricity will go down the wire into the vial, and the inside of the vial have a good deal of electricity in it.

Then the cylinder is no longer turned, and the vial is set on a table.

If any body touches the bottom of the vial, with one hand, and, then, brings the other hand very near to the brass ball of the vial, he will instantly feel a hard shock in his wrists, elbows, and breast, as if somebody had struck him. The electricity goes, as quick as lightning, from the brass ball, through the person who touches it.

If one hundred, or more, persons should take hold of each others' hands, and stand round in a ring; and the person, at one end, should touch the bottom of the vial with his hand, and the person, at the other end of the ring, touch the brass ball of the vial with his hand, all the persons would, instantly, feel the shock, at the same time. For the electricity would go through them all, from the brass ball, as quick as lightning.

Many such vials are sometimes made, and placed near each other, so that they can all be filled with electricity. They are all connected with each other, so that the electricity can be taken from them all, *at the same time*. There is a way of doing this, without having it pass through any body, and when it is done, there is a prodigious flash, like lightning, and a noise like that of a cannon, when it is fired. These vials, thus put together, are called an *electrical battery;* and, when the electricity is taken from them all, at once, it is called *discharging the battery*.

Just, as when a man loads a gun, he is said to *charge* it, and when he fires it off, to *discharge* it.

R. If the electrical battery should be discharged through a person, it would kill him,—would it not, mother?

M. It might easily be made to do so, my son, if there were vials enough, and if they were filled with electricity.

R. I think, I know, mother, why the fish that you were going to tell me about, is called an *electrical eel.*

M. Well, why is it called so, Robert?

M. Electricity comes from it, mother, when you touch it, just as it does from the electrical battery.

M. You are right, my son, it does so.

Some of these fish have been caught, and kept in vessels, and a great many experiments tried with them. It has been found, that they can give a shock to any person, or animal, that touches, or comes near them; that they can do this, or not, just as they choose; that they can give a small shock, or a hard one; and that the shock is just like that which comes from an electrical vial.

R. Does any spark come from the eel, mother?

M. A spark was seen to come from one, when it was out of the water, and the electricity was discharged from it; but when the fish is under water, no spark can be seen.

These electrical eels have been examined, to see how they are made inside. It is found, that more than one third of the whole fish, is a *curious, electrical battery;* as truly so, as the electrical vials are, though it is made very differently from them.

I cannot, now, describe it to you. It would take too long a time, and I could not do it without a drawing for you to look at, to see the different parts.

There are a great many of these parts, much more curiously made, and put together, than the parts of an electrical machine are; and, as I told you, one of the largest kind of these electrical eels, can *charge his battery* so full, and *discharge* it with so much force, as to kill a man, as quickly as a powerful stroke of lightning would.

Nobody knows, how the fish makes the electricity, inside of him, and charges his battery with it; or how he discharges his battery, so as to give a shock just when he chooses, and as light, or as heavy a one as he chooses.

I will take you, soon, to see an electrical machine, and some of the wonderful effects of electricity.

R. But I do not wish to take a shock, mother.

M. A slight one would not hurt you. You may do as you choose, however.

You will see in the electrical machine, and the vial, and the battery, and some other things to try experiments with, a great deal of design, contrivance, and skill.

R. I am sure I shall, mother; and I shall think, too, all the while, that the electricity made by the machine is the same as that in the clouds,—and that the sparks are like the lightning. I shall be a little afraid of it.

M. It has taken many wise men, a great many years, to find out what we know about electricity; and to make electrical machines; and to know how to charge the vials and batteries, and to use them without danger.

And did chance make the electrical eel ;—with its battery inside of it, ready to be used, at all times, as it chooses, to defend itself against its enemies, or to aid it, in seizing other fish for food ?

And did the fish find out, by chance, too, that it can make electricity, and charge its battery and use it; and did chance teach it, *what to use it for ?*

There are only five different kinds of fishes, that are known to have this power of making and using electricity.

It is a wonderful power for them to have. They can make and use *that something*, which is often so terrible in the dark storm that passes over our heads. How we, sometimes, start at the flash of lightning, and shrink back as the thunder roars around us. It is then, that God seems to show us his great power.

He bows the heavens, and comes down.

Darkness is under his feet.

He flies upon the wings of the wind.

Dark waters, and thick clouds, cover him round about.

God thunders in the heavens.

The Highest gives his voice.

At such times, the atheist has been known to shudder, and tremble, at the power of God, and to cry, and pray, for deliverance from danger.

Let us admire the same power of God, which can so curiously confine, within the body of a small fish, *that electricity*, which gives the thunder-storm its terror. Coming from the clouds, it splits the tallest trees, and destroys animals, and men, and houses. In the body of the fish, and used for his safety and benefit, it can do but little harm.

But only think, if all fishes, and birds, and beasts, and men, had this same power; or if, even all angry men had it!

R. I do not think, mother, that any of us would live a great while.

M. You see, then, my son, in the fish which I have been explaining to you, and in a few others of the same kind, one more striking proof of the power, the wisdom, and the goodness, of God.

R. Yes, mother; and I am sure I shall always remember it, it is so wonderful, and so different from any thing that I have ever heard before.

DIALOGUE XIV.

Robert. Mother, I was stung by a bee, this morning; see how my finger is swelled.

Mother. Not a great deal, Robert. I am glad, it is no worse.

R. I think, I went rather too near the hive. I shall not go so near again.

M. It is best to be careful, my son; for, sometimes, the sting of a bee is very painful, indeed, and it takes a good while to heal the wound.

R. How can such a little insect make so bad a wound, mother?

M. It has a part of its body made for this very purpose.

The sting is inside of a horny sheath, or scabbard. This sheath ends in a sharp point, which is slit, so as to open and let the sting come out, when the wound is made. The sting is double, made of two small darts, very sharp, and barbed like a fish-hook. Each dart has many of these little barbs. One dart is somewhat longer than the other.

Here is a drawing of the sting of a bee, very greatly magnified.

ON NATURAL THEOLOGY.

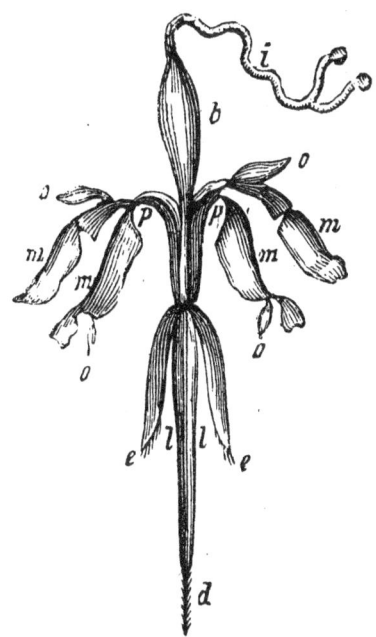

When a bee stings any body, it first pushes the pointed, horny sheath through the skin, into the flesh. Then it thrusts out the longest dart of its sting, through the sheath, into the flesh, where it holds fast with its barbed point. The other dart follows, and so the two darts, one after the other, keep piercing into the flesh, till the whole sting is buried in it.

R. I do not wonder, mother, that the sting of a bee is so painful, and the wound which it makes, so bad.

M. But it would not be so, Robert, if the little insect did not do something more than I have told you.

R. What is that, mother?

M. While the sting is in the flesh, it pours some poison through the sheath into the wound; and it is this which makes the painful swelling. If this was not done, the sting of a bee would be no worse than a pretty deep prick of a pin, or when you cut yourself, a very little, with the sharp point of a pen-knife.

R. Where does the poison come from, mother?

M. There is a little bag, at the root of the sting, which holds it; and there are several curious muscles, with which the bee can move its sting different ways, and thrust it into the flesh, and make the poison flow from the bag, through the sheath, into the wound.

Look, again, at the drawing of the sting, and I will explain to you the different parts.

(i) is the tube in which the poison is made, and which conveys it into the bag (b), from which it is carried, through another tube, into the sting's sheath (ll).

(ee) is the outward sheath, which shuts over the inward sheath ($l\ l$).

($m\ m\ m\ m$) are four cartilages, and ($o\ o\ o\ o$) four, very small muscles, by the help of which, the bee can move the sting different ways.

($p\ p$) are two muscles, to draw the sting into the sheath.

(d) is the sting divided into two parts, and barbed at the sides.

ON NATURAL THEOLOGY.

See, how this little insect is provided with a weapon, sufficient to defend itself against very large, and powerful enemies. It knows very well, too, *how to use it;* and a swarm of bees are as safe against the attacks of animals, as they could wish to be.

R. Yes, mother, I remember, how the bear that tried to get the honey in a beehive, was stung by the bees. I read about it in my book of fables.

The instruments, also, with which the bee and other insects get their food, are very curious, and show us the design, contrivance, and skill of that wise and good Being, who made the little bees, and all other insects; and who constantly takes care of them, as well as of man, and of the larger animals.

R. Do tell me about them, mother.

M. I will; but I must first tell you about a few other things, so that you may understand me the better.

Some persons have taken great pains to find out the different kinds of insects; and how they are made, and how they live, and what they do. They have made large collections of them; and where such a collection is made, and the insects are all put in order, in glass cases, it is called a *cabinet of insects.*

In some of these cabinets there are forty thousand different kinds of insects; but, probably, there are a great many more in the world, which have not yet been discovered.

The manner in which their mouths, and their instruments for getting food, are made, is more curious than that of beasts, birds, or fishes.

Some insects have *jaws;* and, usually, two pairs of jaws, an upper and a lower pair. They do not move against each other, up and down, as ours do, but sideways. The upper pair, in most cases, seize the food, and chew it. The under pair, which are often hooked, hold the food, and tear it, and afterwards, the upper pair make it very fine, before it is swallowed.

The jaws of some are sharp, and are set with little thorns, for tearing flesh; others are hooked, for seizing worms or insects, and, at the same time, hollow, for sucking up their juices;—some cut leaves, like scissors;—others are strong enough to grind the hardest wood between them.

To a great many insects, jaws would have been useless. All the food which they take, is liquid. Moths and butterflies are of this kind. They eat nothing but honey, which is often quite deep, at the bottom of flowers. They need some way, then, of being able to reach it; just as we need some way of getting water from the bottom of a well, before we can drink it.

God has furnished them with just what they need.
They have a slender tongue, hollow inside, like a tube, and sometimes three inches long, which,

when they do not use it, they coil up in a small space, that it may not be in the way, or get injured.

When they use it, they unroll it instantly, and darting it into the bottom of a flower, draw up the sweet juice or honey, on which they feed.

This tongue is a hard kind of flesh, made up of a great many little rings, which lie one above the other, and are moved by an equal number of muscles.

Though it looks very simple, and as if it were only one tube, it is, in fact, made up of three, smaller, distinct tubes; the two outside ones to draw in the air, and the middle one to suck up the honey. This middle tube is nearly square, and formed by the two outside ones coming close together, with a channel, or trough, cut in each.

These two outside tubes are held fast together by a great many little hooks on each, that hook into each other; somewhat as you can hook the fingers of one hand, on to the other, and hold the hands very tight together.

The insect can unhook these outside tubes, or hook them together again, whenever it pleases.

When they are hooked together, *the inside tube is air tight;* that is, no air can possibly pass through its sides. When the insect puts this tube down into the honey, and sucks up the air that is inside of the tube, the air at the bottom of the flower presses the honey up into the tube, and up into the mouth of the insect.

R. Oh! mother, this is like what the boys sometimes do, when they suck up new cider out of the tub, with a straw.

M. It is, my son, and a common pump does something like it, too. The honey is pressed up, by the air, into the tube of the insect, *because there is no air inside of the tube to press the honey down;*—the insect having emptied the inside of the tube of all the air.

For the same reason, the cider rises in the straw, and the water in the pump. You recollect, I explained to you about this *pressure of the air*, when you told me about the sucker which the boys made, and I showed you, that it was like the trunk of the elephant, lifting a heavy weight.

R. I remember it, mother, but I did not think, then, that little insects, like a moth, and a butterfly, have a trunk, too.

M. And quite as curious a one, you see, Robert, as that of the great elephant.

It was a long, long while before men found out how to make a pump; and I dare say, the man who made *the first one*, was thought to have a great deal of design, contrivance, and skill; and if any body had said, that it was not made by the man, but *came by chance*, one day, the people would have laughed at him, as a very foolish man.

Who contrived and made its little pump for the butterfly, which is, indeed, much more curious than our pump in the well is? Did no one make it; no one design it for any particular use? Did all its parts happen to *come together by chance*—not only in one butterfly, but in the millions and millions of butterflies that have lived; and did they happen to come together, just *exactly right*, and always *exactly alike*, so as to make the same kind of pump, for hundreds and hundreds of years?

For there was a time, my son, when *the first butterfly* lived, and laid its little eggs.

R. Oh! yes, mother, just like the *first hen*, about which you told me, and then more butterflies came out of the eggs, and so there have been millions, and millions of butterflies in the world.

M. But there is a great difference, Robert, between the eggs of a hen, and those of a butterfly.

R. I know that, mother; I never saw the eggs of a butterfly, but they must be a great deal smaller than those of a hen.

M. Yes, some of them are not larger than the head of a pin, and they are very different in another respect. Little chickens come out of the eggs which the hen lays; but little butterflies do not come out of the eggs which the butterfly lays.

The eggs of the butterfly are laid on the leaf of some plant, very often on the leaf of a cabbage, and stuck fast to it, with something like glue, where they remain some weeks, and sometimes months, before they are hatched. The butterfly takes no care of the eggs; indeed, she dies very soon after laying them. They are hatched by the warmth of the air, and heat of the sun, and, at last, out of each egg comes—a *worm-like caterpillar.*

This caterpillar crawls upon sixteen short legs, and has two jaws, with which it greedily devours leaves.

It has twelve eyes, so very small that they cannot be seen without a microscope.

It eats the leaves of the plant on which the egg was laid, very voraciously, and grows faster than almost any other animal. It grows so fast, that its skin becomes too tight; and it bursts through it, and casts it off, and very soon has a new skin. This it does, five or six times.

After some weeks, or in some kinds of caterpillars, some months, this little animal begins to get ready for another singular change.

It may be seen crawling away from the plant on which it has fed, and trying to find some place, out of sight, where it may be safe from its enemies. For, pretty soon, it will stop eating entirely, and not be able to move, or help, or defend, itself.

It often climbs up high walls, and gates, and trees, to find such a place as it needs.

Having found it, the caterpillar spins from its mouth a great many, very fine, silken threads, by which it hangs from some projection, or from the underside of a leaf or branch. Some kinds hang with the head downwards; while others hangs sideways, by means of a silken belt, which they make round the middle of their bodies.

It now begins to try to force itself, once more, out of its skin; which, after a great deal of twisting, and struggling, it at last, succeeds in doing. But, sometimes, this is so difficult, that it takes a day or two, to accomplish it.

Out of the old skin, there comes a little animal, very different from the caterpillar, and it is called, a *chrysalis.*

This chrysalis has little hooks on its tail, with which it fastens itself to something like a small, silk button, which the caterpillar spun, to hang upon.

It now tries to get the old skin of the caterpillar out of the way; putting itself in all sorts of shapes; pushing against the old skin; and spinning itself round, with a sudden jerk, fifteen or twenty times. At last, it succeeds; the old skin is cast away; and there hangs the chrysalis, waiting for another, and still more astonishing change.

Here is a drawing of a caterpillar (*a*), and of a chrysalis (*d*), hanging as I have just been explaining to you.

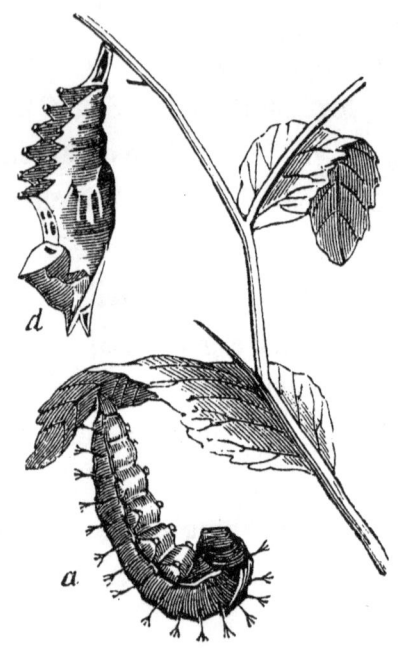

The shape of the chrysalis is quite different from that of the caterpillar. It is the *case* which holds the insect that is soon to come out of it; and inside of this case, all the parts of the insect are curiously and carefully folded up.

The chrysalis seems hardly to be alive. It keeps hanging from the silk button, and does not move, nor eat. It continues so, sometimes, for weeks; and sometimes, for months; and sometimes, for a year, or more; according to the season when the eggs were laid and hatched, and the time that the caterpillar was growing, and the size of the insect that is to come out of the chrysalis.

At length, the time comes, for the insect to burst its prison-house. It begins to struggle to escape. The skin is rent, and, opening wider and wider, out comes a beautiful, winged butterfly.

This gay, happy insect, glitters in the sunbeam, and floats on the breeze, and sports from flower to flower, and sips the delicious honey, a few summer days, or at most, weeks, and then dies. Before it dies, however, it lays its eggs, from which, in the same way, new caterpillars, and chrysales, and butterflies are again to come; all having their various parts formed with perfect exactness, and, in each state, perfectly alike; egg like egg,—caterpillar like caterpillar,—chrysalis like chrysalis,—butterfly like butterfly,—year after year, from *the first butterfly* down to the last one that has lived.

What design, what contrivance, what skill! No man can imitate it. *God alone has wisdom and power sufficient to do it.* And every beautiful butterfly that you see in your walks, in the fields, tells you, as if you should hear a voice from heaven; *There is a God, who made, and preserves, and governs, all beings and things.*

Before we go, I wish to say one thing more to you, about the butterfly.

What wonderful changes take place in this little animal, from the time that it is in the egg, to the day when it bursts its tomb, and comes forth, no more to crawl on the ground, or to hang lifeless from the branch of a tree, but to fly, freely and joyfully, through the air.

Who could have thought such a change possible, if some one had not found it out, by actually seeing it?

But God made this change, and his wisdom and power can make still more wonderful changes.

He tells us, in the Bible, that these bodies of ours, which must be laid in the grave, and there moulder away to dust, will again come forth—more surprisingly changed than the brilliant butterfly is, when it leaves its confinement.

If we love and obey God, and trust in that Savior, who himself burst the bars of the tomb, and rose from the dead, and is gone to Heaven, we too, shall rise joyfully from the grave, and *our bodies will become like unto Christ's glorious body.*

We shall all be changed in a moment, in the twinkling of an eye, at the last trump; (for the trumpet shall sound;) and the dead shall be raised incorruptible, and we shall be changed.

For this corruptible must put on incorruption, and this mortal must put on immortality.

It is the Bible, my son, which teaches us these wonderful truths. And while you admire the wisdom and power of God in the curious butterfly which he has formed, think of *that resurrection from the dead*, which, if you truly love God, will so change your present feeble and decaying body, that *it will live in immortal health, and youth, and strength, and beauty.*

DIALOGUE XV.

ROBERT. You told me, mother, that there is a kind of butterfly, which lays its eggs upon the leaf of a cabbage, and that the caterpillar, which comes from the egg, eats the leaf of the cabbage for its food. How did the butterfly know, that the cabbage-leaf would be the right kind of food for the caterpillar?

MOTHER. I am glad, Robert, to hear you ask me such a question, for it shows that you have been thinking about what I have told you. Try, as much as you can, to find out the *reason of things*. Sometimes, you will be able to do this, *yourself*, and the oftener you can do so, the better; for every time that you succeed, you will be encouraged, and your mind will be strengthened, to *try again*, and, perhaps, to succeed again.

R. *I have tried*, mother, to find out the reason, why the butterfly always lays its eggs on the right kind of leaf, but I cannot, and so I have asked you to tell me.

M. It certainly is strange, my son, that the butterfly should always do so, and never make any mistake; for you know it lays its eggs but once, and dies soon after, so that *it could not have learned, by doing it several times*, where the proper place is, for its eggs to be hatched. Besides, the butterfly never, itself, eats the cabbage leaf; for it lives on nothing but the sweet honey, which it pumps up from the bottom of the flowers. How, then, should it know, that the caterpillar, which is to come from its egg, will not be able to eat honey, and that its only food must be the cabbage-leaf.

R. Well, mother, I am sure this is strange enough, and I cannot see any reason for it.

M. I too, my son, am filled with wonder, when I think of it; and, I know very little more about it, than you do. I know, that it is so, but *how it is*

ON NATURAL THEOLOGY. 179

so, I shall be able to explain but very little to you.

Different kinds of insects have very different places in which to lay their eggs, and, also, very different ways of doing it.

There is a kind of moth, which lays its eggs in the autumn, and they are not hatched till the spring. If they were placed upon a leaf, the wind in winter might blow them a great way off, and the caterpillar might starve for want of its proper food. So the moth places the eggs round the twigs of the tree, the leaves of which the caterpillar is to eat.

The eggs are in rings, and look like little pearls, and the French gardeners call them *bracelets*. They are glued together, with a kind of gum, which is so hard, that it keeps them from being blown away by the wind, or injured by the rain, or devoured by any insects.

All this the moth contrives to do with its tail, and hind feet.

Does the moth know *the reason* why it does so?

There is a small fly that lays its eggs upon the branches of rose trees, and of other plants, on the leaves of which the caterpillar is to feed. To do this, it makes little cells, or small regular holes, to put the eggs in.

If you had to make these cells, you would have to use a gimblet, to bore the holes, and a file, to make them regular and smooth. But the little fly has no gimblet or file. It has, however, what is quite as good, —an instrument like a saw. This saw is more curious than ours, for it has teeth on each side; so that it is like two saws put together, and can cut both ways, and answer the purpose, both of a gimblet and a file.

Does this fly know, that the caterpillar, that is to come out of the egg, will eat only certain kinds of leaves?

A small gad-fly lays its eggs, to be hatched, in the hides, or skins, of oxen and cows. I dare say, you have seen these insects flying about the oxen, and troubling them very much; for the gad-flies hurt them a good deal, when they pierce the skin of any of the tender parts of their bodies. Does the gad-fly know, that it would not do to lay its eggs on the leaves of plants?

Did you ever see a spy-glass, Robert?

R. Yes, mother; do you not remember the one that uncle John has, which pulls out so many times?

M. Well, the gad-fly has, in its tail, an instrument, hard and tough, like horn, made of four pieces, which draw out, just like the pieces of a spy-glass. At the end of it, there are five pointed hooks, three of which are longer than the rest. These form an instrument very much like a gimblet, with which, in a few seconds, the wound is made, and the eggs laid.

The little ants, which, you know, live together, in great numbers, in their small houses, are very attentive, indeed, in taking care of their eggs. All the eggs are laid by *one of the ants*, which is called, the *queen ant*. She does not lay them in some particular place, but any where about the ant-nest. And she does not take the least care of them herself.

As soon as the eggs are laid, there are other ants, called *workers*, which immediately take them up in their mouths, and keep turning them backward and forward with their tongue, to moisten them.

They lay the eggs in heaps, placing them in different rooms, and constantly take care of them till they are hatched. Frequently, in the course of the day, they remove them from one part of the nest to another, as they may need more or less heat, or more or less moisture.

After the eggs are hatched, which happens in a few days, the workers are very careful of the little worms, or grubs, as they are called. They get them food constantly; and, every day, an hour before sunset, they regularly remove them to little cells, lower down in the earth, where they will be safe from the cold, and in the morning carry them back again. If it is going to be cold or wet, however, they let them remain in the lower cells.

What is very remarkable, the workers do all this,

earlier or later, in the morning and evening, according as the sun rises and sets, earlier or later. For, as soon as the sun shines on the outside of their nest, the ants that are at the top, go below, in great haste, to rouse their companions, and these quickly carry the grubs to the upper part of the nest, where they leave them a quarter of an hour, and then carry them into rooms where the sun cannot shine directly upon them.

Sometimes the older grubs, in one nest, amount to seven or eight thousand, and the younger ones to as many.

The older ones eat the most, and the workers have to work very hard, to supply them with food, which they do, several times a day.

They take great pains, too, to keep the grubs clean, and for this purpose the workers are continually passing their tongues over them.

After the young grubs have fully grown, they wrap themselves up in a silken case, which they spin out of their own bodies, and now they begin to change their appearance and shape, and each one is called a pupa.

These pupæ, inside of the silken cases, which are called, *cocoon*, although they do not eat, require as much care as the grubs did.

Every morning and evening, they are carried up

and down, in the nest, as the eggs were; and if, at any time, the nest is crushed by the foot of some animal which is passing over it, the ants are all busy in picking out the cocoons from the earth, and in putting the nest in order again.

Do the workers know when the pupæ are fully grown, and that it is time for them to come out of the cocoons? Do they know, too, that the pupæ are too weak to do this alone? For, just at the right time, three or four begin to pull off some of the silken threads from one end of the cocoon, to make it thinner. They make several, small openings, and cut the threads, one by one, which separate these openings, till a hole is made, large enough to let the prisoners out.

They do all this, very gently; and then, with equal care, pull off the old skin which is on the pupæ, and watch them for several days, and teach them how to find their way through all the rooms, and windings of the nest.

If I had time, I would tell you a great deal more about these curious and industrious, little insects, and, also about the great variety of ways in which different insects lay their eggs, and provide for their being hatched, and for the caterpillars, and grubs, which come out of the eggs, finding their food.

It is very difficult to find out, *how it is*, that

insects seem to know so well what to do, to take care of themselves, and of their eggs, and of their young.

They do some things, which, it would seem, *they must think beforehand*, how to do. And so do beasts, and birds, and fishes. But, then, all of them do a great many things, very curiously, and exactly, and regularly, without seeming to have the least contrivance, or thought, about it.

Birds of the same kind, build their nests in the same way, year after year. So do bees, their hives; and all the little cells are made as exactly of the right size and shape, as if the bees were able to draw lines and figures on paper, and calculate how it ought to be done, just as a man does, how a house should be built.

Do birds contrive, beforehand, how to build their nests; and bees, how to make their hives? Do the old ones teach the young ones how to do this? If so, it is strange, that they should do so, exactly alike, year after year, and not make some alterations or improvement. It would take a man a good while, to learn to make a bee-hive. He would make a great many mistakes, probably, at first, and have to try a great many times, before he got it exactly right.

R. Yes, mother, and after he had skill enough to

ON NATURAL THEOLOGY.

do it, it would take him a long time, to teach another man how to do it.

M. That is true, Robert; and if he should teach a hundred men how to do it, and they should teach a hundred others; and so on, till a million of men were taught, do you suppose, they would all make their beehives exactly alike, as the bees do?

R. I think not, mother.

M. Besides, my son, it takes a great many bees to make one hive, and yet they all go to work on the same plan. They all work together, without confusion, or mistake. Some do one thing, and some, another; and yet they all do just what ought to be done, at the right time, and in the right place, till the hive is finished. This they do, too, in different countries, and in different years, summer after summer.

If the bees are obliged to learn how to do all this, if they really think, and reason, and talk about it; if they truly make their hives with the *design* of living in them, and of storing away their honey, and of taking care of themselves, and of their eggs and their young; and if they *contrive beforehand*, how to build their hives, and carry on all their business;—then, in these respects, they have more design, contrivance, and skill than men have.

R. And if so, mother, I do not see, why they do not learn to do other things for their comfort; just as when a man has contrived how to make one curious thing, he can easily contrive how to make other curious things.

M. I think so, too, Robert; and as men keep finding out, how to make new and useful things, year after year; and people in some countries grow wiser and more skilful, than they do in some other countries; it would seem as if it would be so among the bees. But it is not; they are just as wise and skilful in one country, as in another; and they are no more so now, than they were thousands of years ago.

And this is true of all the different kinds of insects of fishes, of birds, and of beasts.

Man alone has the power of making new discoveries, and of designing new things; and of improving, year after year, in wisdom and skill. Men, now, have a great many conveniences, and comforts, and advantages, which they did not have, hundreds of years ago.

What a difference there is between the house in which we live, and the wigwam of an Indian; between the clothes which we wear, and the skin of a wild beast which he throws around him. But there is no such difference between the hives of bees, or between the different things which they get for their comfort. They all live, and fare, alike.

Sometimes, people have put some of the eggs of a

duck into a hen's nest to be hatched with her own eggs. After the eggs are hatched, the hen will take as good care of the little ducks, as of her own chickens. As soon as the ducks can get to any water, deep enough to swim in, away they go, and plunge into it, and swim about, with as little fear, and with as much ease, as the old ducks do. This troubles the hen a great deal. She makes a great noise about it, and does not seem to understand, at all, that the little ducks are made very differently from the chickens, with feet on purpose to swim in the water, and that they will have to get their food in a different way from what the chickens will.

R. And the hen does not seem to understand, mother, that the bill of the ducks is very different from that of the chickens. You recollect, you explained it to me.

M. Yes, my son, and I am glad, you have not forgotten it.

You see, the hen does not seem to know any thing about the reason, why the ducks go into the water, and the chickens do not. She tries to keep the ducks from going into it, and, in every way, takes the same care of them and of the chickens, and treats them exactly alike.

Why is she so stupid about this, when she seems to know so much about other things?

And why, too, did the little ducks go so soon into the water? No duck taught them to do so. The hen tried all she could to prevent them from doing it. How did they know that the water would be a good place for them, and that they could swim in it?

R. The more you tell me about these things that animals do, mother, the more strange it seems to me.

M. It is, indeed, strange, my son; and there is no other way of explaining it, but to consider it as *made to be so by God himself*.

R. Do you mean, mother, that God makes the butterfly lay its eggs in the right place; and the ants take care of their eggs, and grubs, and pupæ, as they do; and birds build their nests; and bees, their hives; and little ducks go into the water?

M. I do, my son, though not in the same way in which he makes the wind blow, or the lightning come from the clouds, and strike a tree.

But we have talked a good while, and must stop now. I will talk with you again, about the way in which God makes animals do a great many things, to-morrow morning.

DIALOGUE XVI.

Mother. Well, Robert, have you had a pleasant walk?

Robert. A very pleasant one, mother, and I stopped to see a caterpillar hanging from a silk button, on the under side of a leaf.

M. I cannot think, Robert, that the caterpillar does this, because it knows, that it is about to be turned into a chrysalis, and that, afterwards, the chrysalis will be turned into a butterfly.

R. What, then, makes it do so, mother?

M. I was beginning to explain to you, yesterday, about the way in which God makes the caterpillar do this; and makes other insects, and the fishes, and birds, and beasts, do a great many curious things, for doing which, *they do not seem to understand the reason at all.*

God gives them *different instincts*, which direct them to do certain things, without their being obliged to *learn how to do them*, and without their knowing why they do them.

Even plants seem to have something like instincts.

When a kernel of corn is put into the ground, (or, indeed, the seed of any plant,) after some time, a green sprout comes out from one end of the kernel, and a good many, little, white threads, from the other end. The sprout finds its way *upward* through the earth, and grows, and becomes a stalk of corn, and bears ears.

The little threads run *downward*, and become roots, and help to fix the stalk strongly in the earth, and to draw nourishment for it, from the earth.

Now, what is very curious, is, that you may put the kernel into the ground, either end up, or either side up, any way that you choose, and the sprout will, always, take the right direction, *upward*,—and the little threads, their right direction, *downward*.

R. Mother, did you never see how the bean-vines always go towards the poles, and climb around them?

M. I have, my son, and this, as well as what I have told you the kernel of corn does,—may be considered as an *instinct*. It is done, without the kernel, or the vine, thinking, or knowing, any thing about it.

R. Are there any other, curious instincts in plants, mother?

M. Many, my son. If a vessel of water is placed within six inches of a cucumber vine that is growing,—in twenty-four hours, the vine will change its direction, and not stop till it touches the water.

There is a curious plant, called a *fly-trap*, the leaves of which are jointed, and have two rows of strong prickles on them.

If a fly, or any other insect, alights on these leaves, instantly they rise up; the rows of prickles lock themselves fast together, and the little animal is caught, and soon dies. It is thought, that in some way, the plant is nourished by the dead insect.

Here is a drawing of a part of this curious plant. You see, a little insect has just got caught in its leaves.

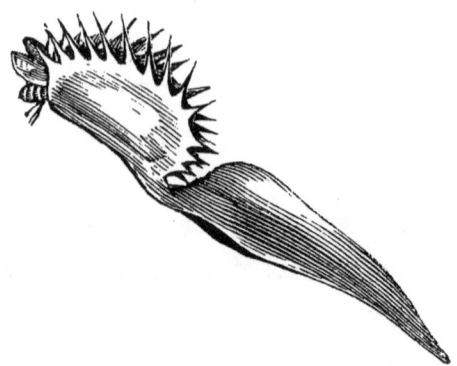

Here, again, is what may be called *instinct*. When the leaves spring together and catch the insect, and do not open till it dies, the plant feels nothing, and knows nothing, of all this, or of the reason why it is done.

R. Mother, has a clock instinct? It strikes, to tell us what o'clock it is.

M. No, my son, we know *how* the clock strikes. The weight makes the wheels go round, and the wheels raise the hammer, and it strikes the bell. We call this *mechanism*. Machines have not instinct.

It is only those things that have vegetable and animal life, which have instinct.

What the cause of instinct is, we do not know, nor in what way God gives it to the plants and animals, and makes it always act as it does, regularly, and without any mistake.

If I move my hand suddenly towards your eyes, as if I were going to strike them, you wink them, instantly.

R. Yes, mother, and I cannot help doing it.

M. A little infant does the same. The reason of doing it, is to protect the eye from injury. But neither you nor the little infant, think of this reason, when you wink your eyes, nor think, at all, about doing it.

It is instinct, that leads you to do so.

It is instinct, that directs different animals to do what they do, to preserve their lives, to defend themselves against danger, to provide for their wants, to build their nests, and other habitations to live in, and to take care of their young.

They do all this, in a very different way from that in which a clock strikes, or a steamboat moves through the water. *For animals are not machines.*

They do it, too, in a very different way from that, in which men learn how to take care of themselves, and of each other, and to invent and make things, for their comfort and improvement.

We cannot suppose, that the birds in building their nests, or the bees in making their hives, learn, first how to do it, and then plan and calculate, and reason about it, as men do, when they build a house, a church, a ship, or a bridge.

We cannot believe, that they have such wonderful wisdom, design, contrivance, and skill. It is instinct which directs them; and, *in this way*, God shows us his great wisdom, and power, and goodness. For he made the *first butterfly* with an instinct, to lay its eggs on the proper leaf; and the *caterpillar*, to eat this leaf, and to hang, just at the right time, from the silk button; and the *chrysalis* to come out from the skin of the caterpillar, and hang, also, from the silk button, and, at last, the *butterfly* to come out from its case, which it has to strive very hard to do, and stretch its wings, and seek its food, and lay its eggs, before it dies.

How wonderful, that these instincts, thus go from the old butterfly to the young ones, and so on, for hundreds and thousands of years.

Think of all the beasts, and birds, and fishes, and insects, that are now living, and that have ever lived;—how many millions, and millions, and millions of them there have been. They have all had their *peculiar instincts*, directing them, in different ways, to do the different things that were necessary for their safety and comfort, and for that of their young.

How these instincts are given to animals, and made to act with so much certainty and accuracy; how they are made to go from the old to their young, and from these to their young again, and so on, we cannot understand, or explain.

God alone, knows, how it is done ; for he does it. And it is, my son, even a more striking proof of his design, contrivance, and skill, than the wonderful way in which he has made the different parts of the bodies of animals, and put them together.

You told me, some time ago, that you should think it would be very wonderful, indeed, if a man could make a watch, so that the wheels should move and move, in such a way, as to have another watch come out from it, as a chicken does from an egg, and another watch from this, and so on, and so on.

But suppose, a man, besides this, could make the first watch, so that it could keep going of itself, for one year, and then tumble all to pieces; but, just before it tumbled to pieces, it should move its wheels, *as if by instinct*, and make another watch like itself, to go as it had done; and, at the end of a year, this watch make another watch, and then, tumble to pieces; and so on, and so on. What would you think of this ?

R. I should think, mother, that the design, contrivance, and skill, of the man were so great, that, if I did not see the watches, I could hardly believe any thing about it.

M. How much greater design, contrivance and

skill, are seen in the instincts of butterflies, and of other animals; so that here is *another kind of proof*, different from any that we have had before, of the existence, wisdom, power, and goodness of God.

R. I shall think of it, mother, when I see a bird building its nest, or the caterpillar spinning its threads.

M. I hope you will, my son, and thus, as you look around you, *see God in all things;* in the little ant beneath your feet, as well as in the larger animals; in *their wonderful instincts*, as well as in their curious bodies, and motions; in the flowers, and plants, and trees; in the gentle breeze, and in the roaring storm; in the glorious sun, by day, and in the beautiful moon and stars, by night.

R. Before we stop talking, mother, I wish to ask you one question.

M. Do, my son, you know, I am always ready to answer your inquiries.

R. Do not animals sometimes think, beforehand, *how* they will do certain things, and *why* they will do them?

M. Yes, Robert, I cannot but think so. They often do things which cannot be explained by mere instinct.

R. Then they are like us, mother.

M. Yes, my son, in some few things; but, after

all, what a vast difference there is between them and us. In one thing, you know, we are entirely different from them. They do not know, neither can they be taught, the least possible thing about God, and the soul, and a future world after death. They have no ideas, or feelings, with regard to what is right and wrong; and when they reason at all, which but very few of them do, in but very few instances, they reason only about some little things, and there stop. Their reason does not seem to improve, and those who seem the wisest of them, know but very little, indeed, except what they know and do, by instinct.

R. Mother, I do not understand exactly, what *reason* is. Will you please to explain it to me?

M. It would take me a long while, Robert, to tell you all about it, but I will tell you enough, to show you, *how very different reason is from instinct.*

If something is coming very suddenly towards your eyes, you shut them; but you do not think that you will do this, or why you will do it. You do it from instinct, or, as we say, *instinctively.*

I have read a story of a lady who was one day walking alone, in a country where tigers live. One of these terrible animals suddenly appeared, and began to approach her. What could she do, to defend herself? In an instant, she thought of one thing, that might possibly drive the tiger away. She had a

parasol in her hand. She opened it suddenly towards the tiger, and he was so frightened by it, that he immediately turned about, and ran off into the woods.

The lady perceived the great danger she was in; she thought *how* she might prevent the tiger from attacking her; she thought *opening the parasol* suddenly towards him, might do this; and she opened the parasol *for this very purpose*.

In doing this, she *reasoned*. She had seen little children, perhaps, or some kinds of animals, startled, by having something come very suddenly towards them. She might have been alarmed herself, some time or other, in this way. She recollected it, and thought, that in the same way, the tiger might be alarmed, by the opening of her parasol.

It was *reason*, and not instinct, that led her to act so wisely.

The caterpillar throws off its old skin, exactly at the right time; not because it thinks that it will have a new, and better one, or that it must do this several times, that, at last, it may be prepared to hang from the silk button, and become a chrysalis, and afterwards, a beautiful butterfly. It knows nothing about these wonderful changes. How can it? It never passed through them before, or saw any other caterpillar pass through them; nor has it ever been taught about them by any other insect. What the caterpillar does, it does, without thinking of the different ways in which it must act, or of the purpose for which it must act. *It acts entirely from instinct.*

When your uncle John takes off his thick woollen coat, in the spring, (as the weather begins to be quite warm,) and lays it away in his trunk, and puts on a thinner one,—he does this, not from instinct, but from *reason.*

He has learned, from having done so before, that it is best for his comfort and health; he thinks, that the cold weather is passed, and that the summer is coming on, and that he shall not need his thick, warm coat again till the autumn, unless it may be, now and then, on a cool day. What he does, he does *on purpose*, and can tell you, *why he does it*. He does it from reason.

Instinct is that something which God gives to animals, so that it is as much a part of them as their life is, which directs them to do certain things to preserve their lives, and to take care of themselves, and of their young, and to continue their different kinds, year after year;—and to do all this, certainly and regularly, without having been taught it,—and with as much skill, the first time, as the second, third, fourth, or at any time, afterwards,—and without thinking, *why it is done.*

Reason is, also, the gift of God. *It is his peculiar gift to man.* It is that which makes man so very different from beasts, birds, fishes, and insects.

You see reason beginning to show itself in a very young child. How soon the child seems to learn both *how*, and *why*, to do certain things. It soon understands, also, *how*, and *why* other persons do certain things. It early shows *design* in what it does, and sometimes considerable *contrivance* and *skill*.

When it learns to talk, how soon it begins to inquire *how* things are made, and *why* things are made; *how* things are done, and *why* they are done.

The child very early understands *why* it ought to do what is right, and not to do what is wrong; and *how* it ought to conduct towards its parents; and do to others, as it would have others do to it. It continues to improve, and understands *how* and *why*, it must believe that there is a God, who made all beings and things; and *how*, and *why*, it must love, obey, and serve him, that its soul may be prepared, after its body is dead, to go to heaven, and be holy and happy, there for ever. It is *reason* that enables the child to do all this.

But if I should go on to tell you all the things which reason enables children and men to do, I might spend years in telling you.

Whenever we think, *how* any thing was made, or *why* it was made, we *reason*. Whenever we think, *how* a thing might be done, and *why* it would be well to have it done, we *reason*. Whenever we think, *why* we ought to conduct in a certain way, so as to do right,—or not to conduct in a certain way, so as not to do wrong, we *reason*. Whenever we think, *how*, or *why*, any thing will make us and others, more wise, or good, or happy,—or less so, —we *reason*.

And, because our minds, or souls, are able to do

all this, we say they have reason, and that *reason enables them to do it.*

R. Mother, how glad I am, that I have reason.

M. That you may well be, my son. When you see the little birds, and insects, doing many curious things, *the wonderful instincts* which direct them to do these things, show you that there is a God. But how much more striking is the proof, that there is a God, when you see children, and grown people, doing those things which are so far, *far above instinct*, and which *reason alone* enables them to do.

How did man get this wonderful power of his soul? Whence came his soul itself? How came it to be united to his body?

You have seen how our *bodies alone*, from the design, contrivance, and skill, with which they are made, and their different parts put together, and kept in order, prove that there is a God. How much more, then, do our *souls* prove this; with powers so superior to those of the body; with reason so superior to the instincts of the brutes; with reason, *the peculiar gift of God to man, and which makes man somewhat like God.*

How thankful, my son, should you be to God, for giving you reason. And how careful should you be, so to use your reason, that you may continue to improve in knowledge and goodness,—that you may

make others and yourself, wiser, better, and happier,
—that you may become *more and more like God*,
and thus be prepared to know more of him, in heaven, and to be happy, in loving and serving him,
for ever.

DIALOGUE XVII.

ROBERT. Mother, uncle John has made me a
new bat to play ball with, out of a hard piece of
wood, and it is the best bat that I ever had.

MOTHER. Suppose he had made it a foot longer,
how would you like it then?

R. It would not do for me, mother. I should
think, then, that uncle John had made it for himself.

M. Yes, your uncle John needs a longer bat to
play ball with, than you do; and a little boy would
need a shorter bat,—so that the bat must be suited
to the height of the person. This we call *proportion*.
And if your bat just suits your height, we say that
the proportion between the length of the bat, and the
height of your body, is right. Do you not think,

your uncle John thought of this proportion, when he made your bat?

R. I am sure he did, mother; for before he cut it off, he asked me several times, to take hold of it at the right place, and see how long it ought to be.

M. He had a *design*, then, in making it of just the length that he did. Do you suppose that the man who made the chairs in this room, had a *design* in making them just as high as they are?

R. Certainly he had, mother. He made them for men and women to sit on, and that small, low chair, he made for a little boy or girl to sit on.

M. Did you ever think, my son, how our houses and furniture, and all the different kinds of things which we use to work with, *are proportioned to the size of men and women, and to the use which we make of them.*

R. I never did before, mother, but now that you have told me, I see that it is so.

M. If you should see a house with doors only half as high and wide as the doors of our house; and windows half as large; and go inside, and find every thing in the same proportion—all the tables, and chairs, and beds, and things to be used, just half the size of ours, what would you think?

R. I should think, the house, and all the things in

it, were made for people, only half as large, and tall, as you and uncle John are.

M. Yes; and that would certainly appear to be the *design* of the person who contrived the house, and had it built, and the things made and put into it.

Proportion, then, between the different parts of a thing, or between one thing and others, is one way in which we see proofs of design, contrivance, and skill.

R. Mother, I have just thought, if my arms were as long as uncle John's, or his arms as short as mine, how inconvenient it would be.

M. True, my son, and only think how all the parts of your body, are not only suited, but exactly proportioned, to each other.

How clumsy a head would be, two or three times larger than the one you now have. It would require stronger muscles to move it about, and a stronger neck to support it. And, if your legs were twice as long as they are, how awkward many of your motions would be, and how hard it would be for you to bend down and stoop, and pick up things. Your arms, then, would have to be longer, to have the right proportion; and, indeed, all the parts of your body would have to be larger, so as to have one suited to the other.

Think, too, of the proportion between our bodies, and the things and beings around us.

R. I do not exactly understand you, mother.

M. I will explain to you what I mean.—Suppose our cows were two or three times taller than they are, would it not be very inconvenient?

R. It would be, indeed. I do not see, how they could be milked.

M. Well, Robert, there is a *suitable proportion* between them, and the size of men and women.

And so it is with the horse, that animal which is of the greatest use to man. If horses were two or three times taller than they are, it would be almost impossible to ride on horseback; and, if we used them in carts, and wagons, and chaises, and stages, these would have to be made larger, and higher, and very differently from what they are now. What would the farmer do, when he ploughed his field? It would give him a great deal of trouble.

R. And so it would, the hostler, mother, to take care of them.

M. And if our dogs and cats were as big as horses and cows, we could not let them come into our houses.

R. And, besides, mother, how could the cats catch rats and mice.

M. You see, my son, there is a proportion between the size of man, and that of the animals which are intended for his use. And you will see a *similar proportion*, too, between the different kinds of animals, of beasts, of birds, of fishes, of insects, and of plants.

A great many animals live on grass and plants of different kinds; and their shape and size and height are such, and their head, and body, and limbs, so proportioned, that they can get their food without difficulty.

Other animals prey upon different kinds of animals, for food; and their size, and their strength, and their means of securing their prey, are *proportioned to this object*. If mice were obliged to catch cats for food; or the deer, to catch the lion; or flies, to catch spiders; or insects, to catch the birds;—they would soon starve.

How easily, too, all our food is obtained. We eat the flesh of animals; and we have the knowledge and the skill necessary, to provide this kind of food, although we are not so strong as many of the animals which we use for food. The *proportion*, here, is not between our size and theirs, or between our strength and theirs, but between our knowledge, and contrivance, and skill, and theirs. In these respects, we are greatly their superiors, and if it were not so, there are many of them which we could not procure for food.

We eat fruit, too, and vegetables; and our great

article of food, bread, is procured from grain. How well adapted the size of the vegetables is, to our size. If they were much smaller, or if they were a great deal larger, it would be difficult to cultivate them, and to gather them in, at the proper season, and take care of them.

If potatoes were no larger than peas, and had to be planted, and hoed, as they now are, it would be very fatiguing indeed, to do it, and they would hardly be worth raising. And if wheat, and rye, and oats, grew five or six feet high, and with a larger stalk, men would not be tall enough to reap them, or at any rate, it would be a very difficult, and troublesome task. Most of the pleasantest, and most common fruits, can be gathered with the hand, and held in it, while we are eating them. *There is a proportion between them and our hands.*

R. Yes, mother, and I was thinking how awkward, and incovenient it would be, if apples and pears were as large as pumpkins.

M. There is a proper proportion, also, between the size of animals, and that of their young. If the little birds, that come out of the eggs, were as large as the old ones, or if they grew much faster than they do, the nest would not be large enough for them, and they would require so much food, that it would be very difficult for the old ones to take care of them.

R. Mother, I have just thought about another instinct that birds must have.

M. What is that, my son?

R. That which directs them to make their nests, of the right proportion for the size of their eggs, and of the little birds which are to come out of them.

M. Yes, Robert, that is a striking instance of right proportion, and of a curious instinct, at the same time.

You see a similar instance of proportion, and of instinct, in the sizes and accommcdations of all the nests, and hives, and places, which animals prepare for their own comfort, and that of their young.

Who gave them this nice *instinct of proportion?* How happens it to be so certain, so regular, and so universal? Does *chance* produce exact and suitable proportions? Suppose your uncle John should write a letter to a tailor, who never saw him, to have a suit of clothes made, and should not send any measure; and the tailor should not know, whether he was a tall or a short man, a large, or a small one. The clothes might possibly chance to fit, and be proportioned to your uncle John's size and shape. But it would be a mere chance. The tailor might try a thousand times, before he would make the suit of clothes to fit exactly.

But suppose he had to make suits, in the same way,

without any measures, for a thousand men. How many, then, would their clothes exactly fit? It would be a wonder if the proportion was right, even in one instance.

But millions of birds and insects have made their nests, and hives, of the right proportion, for their own comfort, and that of their eggs and young, without taking any measure beforehand, or making any calculation, or, indeed, thinking at all about this proportion.

How could they do this, unless God had given them the *instinct of proportion?*

This instinct proves, that there is a God; and *this, and all the other instances of proportion*, which you see in your own body, and in that of animals, and of plants, and in the size, and height, and shape of men, and animals, and plants, with regard to each other, all show the great wisdom, power, and goodness of God.

When you make a kite, or a bat, or any thing else; you know how much you have to think, and how careful you have to be, to get all the proportions exactly right.

And if you could see a person cutting out a statue from a large block of marble, and giving it size and shape, and all the *nice proportions*, so as to make it look just like a human body, you would greatly admire the *design, contrivance, and skill, of the statuary.*

And if you could see the great church of St. Peter's at Rome, more than 700 feet in length, and 500 in breadth, with its immense dome, rising to the height of 400 feet; and all its beautiful and grand parts, both without and within; and the *exact proportions* between these parts and the whole building; what would you think of the *design and contrivance* of the architect who planned this vast temple, and of the *skill* of those who built it?

But look at what God has wrought. *What beautiful proportions* in the stem, the branches, the leaves, the buds, the flowers of the rose bush; in the head, the body, the wings, the feathers, the feet of birds; in the head, the horns, the neck, the body, and the limbs, of the deer; and above all, in the size and shape, and parts, of the human frame! *What useful proportions*, too, in ourselves and in all the beings and things with which we are acquainted! What *beautiful and grand proportions*, in the hills, and valleys and plains, and rivers, and trees, and plants, that fill the landscapes which are spread around us! And astronomy would show you *still more magnificent and sublime proportions*, between this earth, on which we live, and that sun around which it revolves, and the moon and planets, and the hosts of stars; proportions of shape, and size, and weight, and distance, and attraction,—which would fill you with admiration and awe.

God is the great statuary, who has moulded and formed all the things and beings which you see.

God is the great architect, who has built this world, and all worlds.

God has made all those useful, and beautiful, and grand proportions, of which this world, and all worlds are full.

Whenever, you admire, or wonder at these proportions, think of the Author of them. Think of his wisdom, and power, which could design and make them. This wisdom and power are infinite. Think of his goodness, which has thus furnished you with a constant source of the purest enjoyment, in looking at the thousand beautiful, and grand objects which surround you.

In this way, every thing that is lovely, will have a new loveliness; and every thing that is grand, a new grandeur; because you will feel, that they were thus made, to promote our happiness, by our Father who is in heaven.

DIALOGUE XVIII.

Mother. I told you yesterday, Robert, something about the *proportions* between ourselves, and the different beings and things which surround us There is another subject, something like this, which also shows us the great wisdom, power, and goodness of God.

Robert. Will you be so good, mother, as to explain it to me.

M. I will endeavor to do it.

You know, all animals breathe, and if they did not, they could not live. The air which they draw in, goes to the lungs; (that part of the body by which we breathe;) and there it meets the blood, which also goes to the lungs, from the heart. The air causes some change in the blood, which, after being thus changed, goes back again to the heart, and is sent to all parts of the body. If the blood did not receive this change from the air, it would not nourish and give life to all the parts of the body, as it does.

The heart and the lungs are very curiously made, and so are the arteries, which, like tubes, carry the blood all over the body, from the heart: and the veins, which like tubes, also, carry it back again. You know, when the heart ceases to beat, and the lungs to breathe, a person dies.

R. Do explain to me, mother, how the heart and lungs are made; as you did about the muscles and nerves.

M. I intend to do it, at some future time, my son, and to show you all the pictures which are necessary to your understanding it.

At present, it will be enough for you to know that the lungs are made on purpose to breathe with, and that the heart is made on purpose to send the blood to the lungs, and after the blood has received its change there, to send it throughout the whole body.

The lungs would be of no use without the heart, nor the heart without the lungs; and neither would be of any use, if there were no air for the lungs to breathe, or no blood to be prepared by the air, to give nourishment and life to the whole body.

The air is just what is needed for the lungs to breathe, and the lungs are made exactly to breathe the air.

Here is another striking instance of design, contrivance, and skill, in thus *making one thing suit another*, which is called *adaptation*.

R. Do fishes breathe, mother?

M. They do, my son. They breathe with their gills,

R. But how can they breathe air, when they are under the water?

M. The water is drawn in at the mouth of the fish, and sent to the gills, where a certain portion of air which is in the water, changes the blood, which is also sent to the gills, from the heart.

R. The gills, then, mother, are the lungs of fishes.

M. They are so, my son; and the leaves of trees and plants, are *their lungs*, by which they derive from the air something which is necessary, for their growth and life. Plants, as well as animals, cannot live without air.

R. Have little insects lungs, mother?

M. They have not, my son, any lungs which are like those of men, beasts, birds, or fishes. But there are tubes, or wind-pipes, in some insects standing out from different parts of their body, through which they breathe. In others, as is the case in many caterpillars, there are small holes along the sides, through which the air passes.

R. Well, there is a plenty of air, mother, for all the animals and plants.

M. There is so, Robert. The earth, which, you know, is a great ball, is entirely surrounded with air; and all this air is called the *atmosphere*. It has weight; and the whole atmosphere presses on the surface of the earth with as much force, as water would, if it were all round the earth, to the height of thirty-four feet.

R. How much heavier is water than air, mother?

M. About eight hundred times. But there are some other things about the air, that show how wonderfully it is adapted to certain parts of our body, which I wish to explain to you.

You know, we hear sounds through the ear. Inside of the ear, there is a thin skin, called the *drum of the ear*, with four little bones near it, so made, that when the drum of the ear vibrates, all the bones are put in motion.

R. Mother, what does *vibrate* mean?

M. See, I am going to stick my penknife, a little way into this piece of wood, so that it will stand up straight. Now, I will strike the top of the knife with my finger.

You see, how the knife moves quickly back and forth. It vibrates.

When you strike the top of a drum, it vibrates, and so does the little drum of the ear.

R. But what strikes the drum of the ear, mother?

M. *The air*. When the clapper of a bell strikes against the side of it, the bell has a great many quick *vibrations*. These vibrations of the bell, make vibrations in the air around it; and these make other vibrations, and these, still wider ones; just as a stone thrown into smooth water, puts the water in motion, and makes a little circle round it, and this circle makes a larger one, and this one still larger, till the water is put in motion for a great distance, and strikes against the little plant that is growing in the water, near the opposite shore, and *puts it in motion.*

So the vibrations of the air, which the vibrations of the bell cause, at last strike against the drum of the ear, and *put it in motion*, and it vibrates.

This vibration of the drum of the ear, makes *the four little bones vibrate.*

The vibration of these bones puts a *watery fluid* in motion, which is in a hollow place, back of the drum of the ear.

The vibrations of the watery fluid, somehow or other, affect the *end of a nerve;* and this nerve, which goes to the brain, carries to it the sensation of sound —and we *hear.*

R. If you had not told me, mother, I am sure, I should not have thought, that there were so many curious parts in my ear, and that so much must be done, before I can hear a single sound.

M. Well, my son, what will the atheist say to all that I have told you about breathing and hearing?

Did the air happen to have just such parts, that, if it can be made to meet the blood which flows through our whole body, it will cause just *that change* in the blood, which is absolutely necessary to nourish the body and keep it alive?

And did the heart happen to come together just so, as to form a curious kind of machine, and every time that the blood is brought back to it by the veins, to send it to the lungs to meet the air, and, after it comes back again, changed by the air, to send it all over the body, to nourish it, and keep it alive?

And did the heart happen to be *so powerful a machine*, that it will keep going, and never get out of order, for seventy or eighty years, when a person lives so long; and do this, too, although it works very hard, all the while, day and night.

For the heart contracts, and so forces the blood out of it, four thousand five hundred times, in one hour. You know you can feel it beat, every time that it contracts.

All the blood that is in the body of a grown person, of common size, weighs about thirty-three pounds, and all this passes through the heart and is sent all over the body, nearly twenty-three times in one hour, or once in a little more than every two minutes and a half. Did chance make this wonderful heart?

Then the lungs *happened to be* just suited, both

to the heart and to the air, so as to bring the air and the blood together, in just the proper quantity, and just at the right time, and *just often enough.* It would not do for the lungs to go too fast for the heart; nor the heart too fast for the lungs. To keep the body in good health, *their motions must be proportioned to each other.*

And did chance make all those parts of the heart, the lungs, and the air; and make them all with the right proportions; and put each together, so as to act without any irregularity and confusion; and set, and keep them, in motion, so as to go exactly right; and thus adapt them to each other?

R. Mother, I think, again, of the text of scripture which you repeated to me.

The fool hath said in his heart, there is no God.

M. I am sure, my son, that you will never be guilty of such folly, after all the proofs which I have given you of the being, the wisdom, the power, and the goodness of God. And if, when you grow up, you meet with any one so foolish and wicked, as to doubt, whether there is a God, you will be able to give him the proofs, that there is, indeed, a great and good Being who made him, and all other beings and things, and perhaps you may be able to convince him of this, and, with the blessing of God, help to make him a better and a happier man.

R. I am sure, mother, I will try to do so, if I ever meet with such a person.

M. I have some other things to tell you about the air, Robert, which will still further show you, how admirably it is adapted to the convenience and comfort of man.

R. There seems, mother, to be as much that is curious and wonderful about the *adaptation* of things to each other, as there is about what you told me of their *proportion* to each other.

M. There is, indeed, and the *air* is one striking instance of it.

If it were not for the air, we could not see different objects as well as we do.

R. Why not, mother? Is it not the sun which gives us light? I do not see how the air can make any difference in that light.

M. Did you ever take a looking-glass, Robert, and hold it so that the sun can shine upon it; and then turn it, so that the shining of the sun upon it, may be cast on the wall of the room?

R. I have, mother, and you know you can make the bright spot move about, all sorts of ways, on the wall.

M. Well, we say, that the looking-glass *reflects* the light of the sun, which shines upon it, on the wall.

Now, suppose, there is a room shut up so tight, that it is quite dark in all parts of it, except some very little streams of light, that come through a few holes in the window-shutter, as big as the head of a pin.

That would not give light enough, for you to see to do any thing in the room.

Suppose you could place several looking-glasses, so as to reflect these streams of light, in different directions; and then, other looking-glasses, to reflect again the light coming from the first; and, then, still more, to keep reflecting the light, in all possible ways; this would scatter the light, so completely, into all parts of the room, and upon all the things in it, that you could see quite well.

The air does something exactly like this. It is made up of millions and millions of little particles. smaller, a great deal smaller, than the point of a pin, —which *reflect the light*, from one to another, in all possible ways, and on all the things that we see, and throughout all places, however large. If the air had not this *power of reflecting light*, we could see nothing, only those things on which the sun shines directly; all other things and places would be in the dark.

All the things, too, which we did see, would be bright, and many of them dazzling in the midst of dark objects around them. How different this would be, from the soft and pleasant light, which is now reflected by the air, upon all those objects upon which the sun does not shine directly. What beautiful colors the landscape has, from this mixture of brighter and softer light. So that *the air is adapted*, you see, not only to scatter light enough in all directions, to enable us to do what is necessary to be done; but it furnishes us, also, with a constant source of enjoyment in beholding beautiful tints and colors, and shades, in all the objects around us.

If I had time, I could show you how the different parts of the eye are made, and put together, so as to receive *the light reflected to it from different objects;* and, to carry this light on the back part of the eye; and there, to form a *most curious little picture* of the things at which we are looking, exactly like them, only thousands of times smaller; and, then, somehow or other, to have this little picture affect a *nerve*, and this nerve affect the *brain*, and thus enable us to see.

R. Mother, I do wish to have the different parts of the eye explained to me.

M. I hope to be able to do it, my son, before a great while, but I cannot do it now. I will tell you, however, some few things more about *seeing*, before we go.

I have shown you, how the air reflects the light, in all directions, and how necessary this is for our convenience, and how much it contributes to our enjoyment. The air is admirably adapted to this purpose.

But *light*, also, is most curiously made; so as to be reflected by the *air*, and received by the *eye*. You know, how very small the particles of air are, that reflect the light; and how small the little hole is in the front of the eye, that receives them; and how small the little picture is, on the back part of the eye, which affects the nerve and the brain, and enables us to see. Now the particles of light are *proportioned to all this*, and to the swiftness with which they move, so as to enable us quickly to see things, even at a very great distance.

Light goes at the rate of 195,000 miles in one second of time, which is faster than a cannon ball goes, by one million, five hundred, and fifty thousand times.

The sun is ninety-five millions of miles from the earth, and yet light comes to us from the sun, in eight minutes, and thirteen seconds.

R. Mother, I cannot think, how quick light goes.

M. That is true, my son, and we cannot think how very, very small the particles of light are. If they were larger than they are, they would injure us very much.

R. How so, mother?

M. If I should toss this thimble very gently, against your face, would it hurt you?

R. I do not think it would, but it would hurt me a good deal, if you should throw it, as hard as you could.

M. So would, even the head of a pin, if I should throw it as hard as I could, into your eye; and if it was shot from a gun, it would destroy the sight of your eye, and might, perhaps, kill you. Think, then, how small, how very, very, very small the particles of light must be so as not to hurt the eye, when they strike it, coming as quick as they do, all the way, from the sun!

If a million of the particles of light, all put together, were as large as a small grain of sand, it would be as dangerous to have them strike the eye, as it would be to have a quantity of sand fired straight into the eye from a cannon.

Now think of all these things; how wonderfully the *air* is made to reflect light; and the *eye*, to receive the light, and enable us to see. Think, too, how the *light itself* is made, with its *very small particles*, so as to be easily reflected by the little particles of the air, like so many little looking-glasses. Think, with what amazing quickness, light comes from distant objects, so as to give us the sight of them, without any pain or injury, because its particles are so small, that we cannot think how small they are!

What a *wonderful adaptation* of different things to each other!

What a *wonderful effect* is produced by this adaptation;—our seeing and knowing, not only what is near us, but objects, also, at a great distance. We can see the *sun*, which is 95,000,000 miles from the earth;—and we can see a *fixed star*, (another sun, for other worlds,) which is more than 5,000,000,000,000 miles from the earth.

In all this, how wonderfully God shows us his infinite power and wisdom; and his great goodness, too, in doing it all, for the convenience, and comfort, of man.

CONCLUSION.

Mrs. Stanhope thought somewhat of explaining to Robert, about the sun, and earth, and moon, and stars, and of thus showing him the *wonderful power of God*, as well as his great wisdom and goodness, in the size, and motions, of the heavenly bodies.

But she thought, on the whole, that it would be better to wait, till he grew a little older, when he would be able to understand it much better.

She expected, too, the next day, to ride with him, to his aunt's, where she intended to stay two or three weeks; so she did not talk with Robert, any more, at that time, about the wisdom, power, and goodness of God, as shown to us, in the beings, and things, which he has made, except that, in the evening, just before he went to bed, she had the following, short conversation with him.

———

Mother. I hope, my son, that you will remember all that I have been telling you, for several days past,—to prove to you that there is a God, and that he is a Being of infinite power, wisdom, and goodness.

Robert. I am sure, mother, that I shall never forget it. It has been, both, so entertaining, and instructive, to me.

M. As you gain more knowledge, Robert, of the different beings, and things, which God has made, you will gain, also, more and more proofs of his existence, and of his amazing power, wisdom, and goodness.

You will, if you live, pursue many studies, and read many books, in which *not even the name of God will be mentioned;* although these studies, and these books, will be full of instances of the most wonderful design, contrivance, and skill, and of the most surprising power, wisdom, and goodness, of God

It is sad to see that it is so, and that men love so little to think, and to converse, and to write, about God,—that great and good Being, who made us, and who made so many things for our improvement and happiness,—and who wishes so much, that we should all love and obey him, and be prepared, when we die, to go and live with him, and be happy in heaven, forever.

But in all your studies, and in all your reading, I hope, you will mark those things very particularly, which show you the design, contrivance, and skill, —the power, wisdom, and goodness, of God; and stop, and think of him, with reverence and awe; with gratitude, and love.

Let it sink deep into your soul, and form a part of your daily thoughts and feelings,—how much kindness God has shown, and is still showing you; how many sources of comfort, and of enjoyment, he gives you; how it grieves him, to see you think, or feel, or act wrong; how he loves to see you *be good* and *do good,* that you may go, after death, to be with him forever,—*continually to improve in knowledge, in holiness, and in happiness.*

Remember, too, with the liveliest feelings of thankfulness, that God has given you another and a *brighter light*, to guide you in the way to heaven, than that which shines upon you, from the works of his hand,—from the beings and the things which he has made.

From *these* you may learn his amazing power, and wisdom, and goodness. But you cannot learn from them, a great deal that it is very important for you to know about God, and your soul, and *whither you will go, and what you will be or do, after death.*

God has been very kind, in giving you *another and a brighter light*, to guide you into the knowledge of these important things.

He has given you the Bible. This holy book, which good men wrote, just as God directed them to write it, tells you all that it is necessary for you to know, with regard to God, and your soul, and your existence after death. The more you study it, the wiser you will grow. The more you love and obey it, the better, and the happier, you will be.

In the Bible we read of Jesus Christ, the Son of God, and the only Savior of sinners. We could learn nothing of this Savior, merely from the things which God has made. These show us, indeed, the power, wisdom, and goodness of God, but not his great love to us, in giving his well-beloved Son to die for sinners, such as we are.

By studying ever so much the wonderful works of God in the natural world around us, we could never find out, how our sins are to be forgiven, or whether *they could be forgiven at all.* How thankful, then, we should be to God for giving us the Bible.

While you ought to form the habit of admiring and loving God, as you notice the workmanship of his hands, in the beings and things which he has made; you ought also to form the habit of daily going to your Bible, that you may learn more and more of Jesus Christ, and of the way of salvation through him.

Unless you feel, my dear son, the need of looking to Christ, and of trusting in him, as your only Savior from the awful punishment which your sins deserve, all the knowledge that you may gain of the *works of nature*, and all the admiration that you may feel of the power, and wisdom, and goodness of God, in those works, will be of no use in preparing you for heaven. You may see, in this way, how great and good a being God is; but his power and goodness both will have to be shown in banishing you forever from his presence, if you do not come to him, with heart-felt sorrow for your sins, imploring his forgiveness on account of what Christ did and suffered, and relying on this Savior alone for acceptance with God.

What a solemn thought, that you may live in this beautiful world which God has made, and see in it, and in the body which he has given you, so many proofs of his existence, of his wisdom, of his power, and of his goodness, and yet fail of having him for your eternal friend!

Ah! my son, I should regret the very interesting conversations which we have had of late on Natural Theology, if I did not hope that, with the blessing of God, and the influences of his Holy Spirit, they would lead you to higher views of his character, and to accept the rich offers of his mercy to you through Jesus Christ.

Go to this Savior, sinner, with penitence, humility and faith. Trust in him with all your heart. Beseech God, for his sake, to give you the Holy Spirit, that you may do this, and that you may henceforth be a true disciple of Christ,—loving and obeying the truths which he has given us in the Bible, —imitating his example,—and devoted to his service.

Then a new beauty and glory will be shed over all the works of nature which surround you. While you admire them as the workmanship of God, they will lead you to look up to him, not only as the great Creator of all things, but as the God and Father of our Lord Jesus Christ; and, *through him*, the source of all your blessings in this life, and of endless happiness beyond the grave.

THE END.

Other Related Titles from Solid Ground

Solid Ground Christian Books is delighted to offer several books from Thomas H. Gallaudet and his friend Horace Hooker. The following books are in print and ready to ship.

THE CHILD'S BOOK ON THE SOUL by Thomas H. Gallaudet is the most remarkable of all the books written by the man known as *The Father of Education to the Deaf in America*. This book addresses the reality of the never-dying soul in words that can be understood by a five year old. It is this book that was used more than any of his others to bring children all over the world to seek the living God.

THE CHILD'S BOOK ON THE FALL by Thomas H. Gallaudet is the sequel to *The Child's Book on the Soul*. It is an outstanding little book that introduces the significance of Genesis 3 at a level that can be understood by a child. This is a powerful book that will magnify the seriousness of sin and the glory of God's grace in the Gospel.

THE CHILD'S BOOK ON REPENTANCE by T.H. Gallaudet is a book that examines the specific area of repentance through the medium of dialogues between a mother and her three children. Once again this is a book that examines a critic issue in a way that can be understood by children. The author does an especially thorough job of exposing the danger of incomplete and false repentance.

THE CHILD'S BOOK ON THE SABBATH by Horace Hooker was one of Gallaudet's closest friends. He here lends his efforts to address an important matter in a most gracious and balanced way. Like his friend, Hooker uses the dialogues between a mother and her three children to address the various doctrinal and practical issues that surround the issue of the Christian view of the Sabbath.

ANOTHER RELATED BOOK WE HOPE TO REPRINT...

THE PRACTICAL SPELLING BOOK WITH READING LESSONS by T.H. Gallaudet and Horace Hooker
Two of the leading Christian educators of the first half of the 19th century joined their efforts to produce a remarkable tool for teaching both spelling and reading. This is a very rare volume that deserves a place in every home-school library, and in every Christian and public school. This will be useful even in teaching English as a second language.

Call us Toll Free at **1-866-789-7423**
Visit our web site at **www.solid-ground-books.com**

Other Solid Ground Titles

In addition to the volume which you hold in your hand, Solid Ground is honored to offer many other uncovered treasure, many for the first time in more than a century:

MARY BUNYAN: *A Tale of Persecution & Faith* by Sallie R. Ford

THE CHILD AT HOME by John S.C. Abbott

THE MOTHER AT HOME by John S.C. Abbott

THE FAMILY AT HOME by Gorham Abbott

SMALL TALKS ON BIG QUESTIONS by Selah Helms & Susan Kahler

OLD PATHS FOR LITTLE FEET by Carol Brandt

REPENTANCE & FAITH TO THE YOUNG by Charles Walker

THE KING'S HIGHWAY: *10 Commandments for the Young* by Richard Newton

HEROES OF THE REFORMATION by Richard Newton

HEROES OF THE EARLY CHURCH by Richard Newton

BIBLE PROMISES by Richard Newton

BIBLE WARNINGS by Richard Newton

BIBLE ANIMALS by Richard Newton

BIBLE JEWELS by Richard Newton

RAYS FROM THE SUN OF RIGHTEOUSNESS by Richard Newton

THE SAFE COMPASS AND HOW IT POINTS by Richard Newton

THE LIFE OF JESUS CHRIST FOR THE YOUNG by R. Newton

FEED MY LAMBS: *Lectures to Children on Vital Subjects* by John Todd

TRUTH MADE SIMPLE by John Todd

JESUS THE WAY by Edward P. Hammond

LECTURES ON THE BIBLE TO THE YOUNG by John Eadie

A MANUAL FOR THE YOUNG by Charles Bridges

ADDRESSES TO YOUNG MEN by Charles Baker

THE ASSURANCE OF FAITH by Louis Berkhof

THE SHORTER CATECHISM ILLUSTRATED by John Whitecross

THE CHURCH MEMBER'S GUIDE by John Angell James

THE SUNDAY SCHOOL TEACHER'S GUIDE by John A. James

DEVOTIONAL LIFE OF THE S.S. TEACHER by J.R. Miller

EARLY PIETY ILLUSTRATED by Gorham Abbott

Call for a complete Catalog at **205-443-0311**

www.ingramcontent.com/pod-product-compliance
Lightning Source LLC
Chambersburg PA
CBHW031140160426
43193CB00008B/203